Why Endure Rheumatism and Arthritis?

Why Endure Rheumatism and Arthritis?

by
CLIFFORD QUICK, MSc, ND, DO

Foreword by DOUGLAS LATTO, MB, ChB, MRCOG

London
GEORGE ALLEN & UNWIN
Boston   Sydney

First published in 1980

GEORGE ALLEN & UNWIN LTD
40 Museum Street, London WC1A 1LU

© Clifford Quick, 1980

British Library Cataloguing in Publication Data

Quick, Clifford
  Why endure rheumatism and arthritis?
  1. Arthritis 2. Rheumatism 3. Naturopathy
  I. Title
  616.7'2 065   RC933   79-40985

  ISBN 0-04-616019-1 ✓

Typeset in 10 on 11 point Times by V & M Graphics, Ltd, Aylesbury, Bucks
and printed in Great Britain
by Billing & Sons Ltd, Guildford, London and Worcester

To my wife, Vivien

Author's Acknowledgements

I wish to express my appreciation to Arthur White, ND, DO, for his continual interest and helpful suggestions at various stages of this book and also to my wife, Vivien, for her constructive criticisms and her help in correcting proofs.

I also wish to thank Professor R. R. Porter and the British Association for Science for permission to use the diagram appearing on page 33.

Foreword

It is a great happiness to me and a privilege to write this preface for Clifford Quick on arthritis and allied diseases. Clifford Quick is an enthusiastic student and an advanced thinker on health and nutrition. He and his wife Vivien have written one of the most popular cookery books called *Everywoman's Wholefood Cook Book* (Thorsons Publishers Ltd).

I have myself been interested in this field for many years and professionally have been concerned with it. I am therefore grateful to the author for sharing his wide experience clinically and in practice of this important subject. He has himself worked actively in this field of medicine for many years. He has brought to bear upon it an acute intellectual awareness of the nature of the problem and the inestimable advantage of dealing with arthritic people needing help. He has, I believe, the insight and imagination to ask the right questions and the honesty in pursuit of the answers to be true to the facts as he finds them. His work will be found to be of great value both to practitioners in this field and to those suffering from arthritis.

The late Major-General Sir Robert McCarrison, CIE, MA, DSc, LLD, FRCP, whose work is well known to Clifford Quick, delivered the three famous Cantor Lectures on nutrition in 1936 before the Royal Society of Arts. The thesis sustained in these lectures is that the greatest single factor in the acquisition and maintenance of good health is a perfectly constituted diet, in other words, man is made up of what he eats.

Few people realise that ninety per cent of all our illnesses are due to faulty nutrition. Rheumatic diseases taken early and treated by a properly constituted diet will melt away like snow off a dyke, and even more advanced cases can be completely cured. Once this is understood the fear of developing rheumatoid arthritis or allied diseases that have run through a few generations of your family no longer haunts you.

These simple truths you will find in Clifford Quick's book and once the fear of the disease and the knowledge of how to reverse these degenerative processes are understood you are well on the way to a permanent cure and also the avoidance of other ailments.

Sir Robert McCarrison, whom I knew well, said to me that the three things he demands of food are

1 it should be grown on healthy soil,
2 it should be eaten whole,
3 it should be eaten fresh.

Sir Robert used to quote Isaiah LV.2, 'Hearken diligently unto me and eat ye that which is good.'

Arthritis and allied diseases cause a vast amount of human suffering and misery for which the patient seldom gets much sympathy.

I wish this book a wide readership. It deserves it.

DOUGLAS LATTO, MB, ChB, MRCOG

Author's Preface

My decision to write this book was based on personal experience of the methods of treatment herein described, first concerning my personal health and secondly as observed in a busy practice over many years as a naturopath and osteopath.

My first occupation after graduation (Bristol University) was in industry as works chemist. After two years in laboratory and works plant my health, which had never been robust, had further deteriorated and I changed to an outdoor occupation hoping that it would improve. While still under the age of thirty I suffered from bronchitis and hay fever and the onset of rheumatic disorder in the form of lumbago, sciatica and, later, severe pains in the upper back and neck due to spondylitis (rheumatism in the spine), which later resulted in brachial neuritis to the extent that at times I could write only for short periods due to pain in the hand and arm. My doctor suggested that I was 'highly strung' – presumably he thought my pains were imaginary!

Eventually I developed a severe throat infection for which my doctor advised tonsillectomy. I replied that the tonsils operation had been performed when I was five years of age, but after a second inspection the doctor said that remnants of the tonsils had grown again and should be removed. Although as far back as I could remember I had suffered from periods of sore throat, I expressed reluctance to submit to surgery, whereupon the doctor advised an all-out attack on my tonsils. For this he gave me a battery of remedies including a throat-spray, a gargle, pills and a paint with which to brush my unfortunate tonsillar remnants. At the end of a month's thorough application of these remedies my condition was worse than before.

At this point a friend introduced me to a naturopath who, after examining me, said that if I wished to rid myself of my ills I should follow conscientiously and persistently a course he advised. I was frankly sceptical. I had been taught that the facts of chemistry and physics could be experimentally verified with exactitude. Could it possibly be otherwise in the highly reputed discipline of medicine? My naturopath declined to argue the matter further, saying, 'You have had a scientific training. If you wish to prove or disprove my words you should make the experiment on yourself. Do exactly as I say for six months and then judge the results.'

I could find no good reason to refuse this challenge and so agreed to follow his directions, whereupon he proceeded to give some explanation of the whys and wherefores of the ways in which I was required to *help myself* in conjunction with his further advice and help.

Happily, I was able to report at the end of the six months that my backaches and stiff and painful neck and shoulders had disappeared and that other ills, including a heavy and noxious state of nasal catarrh, had all improved greatly. My scepticism could no longer be sustained. In succeeding months my improvement continued and ever since I have enjoyed excellent health which to me was quite unknown in my earlier years. Meanwhile, I had learned a lot about the human body and how to maintain it in a state of health.

It was this enlightening experience which later led me to study and qualify as a naturopath and osteopath, leading to membership of the British Naturopathic and Osteopathic Association. Not only did I wish to bring to others the benefits I had experienced myself but I was resolved also to find out how and why orthodox medicine appeared to have gone wrong. I was also determined to test the validity of the claims of the naturopathic school in the treatment of disease. Were their theories and practice something new which had never before been expounded? To answer this question I read medical history and found it very enlightening. Far from being entirely new, many of these truths were known and applied more than twenty-five centuries ago and were subsequently lost, only to be rediscovered and again discarded repeatedly in the course of the centuries, to reappear in modern guise as 'nature cure'.

I also came to understand why this basic knowledge and its practical application has seldom been unreservedly acceptable to the doctors, whether those of ancient times or of the modern medical orthodoxy. Also, it has usually been ignored or neglected by most of the general public. One reason for this neglect is that in order to achieve success in these natural methods of treatment, which deal with the causes of disease and do not merely suppress the effects, it is necessary to undertake appropriate measures of self-help, preferably exercising a certain degree of intelligence and understanding in the process.

For this reason, in Chapters 3 and 4 certain relevant facts of medical history are presented which to a large extent still influence the attitudes and practice of modern medicine. Also, the changing patterns of disease from one period to another are related, in Chapters 5 and 6, to the nature and causes of present-day diseases, and some of the anomalies and fallacies which still persist to confuse and mystify those who seek to understand just what is happening in modern medicine are exposed. In Chapters 7 and 8 certain important facts of anatomy and physiology are explained simply to enable the reader to understand the body's defensive and curative mechanisms in health and disease. In the many medical articles which appear in newspapers, periodicals, digests, etc., and also those features in which readers' questions are answered by an anonymous doctor, the expert's advice to the suffering reader is almost invariably limited to 'Go and see your doctor.'

In contrast with this, the information of a medical nature which I have included in the earlier chapters will, I hope, not only provide interesting reading but also convey an understanding of the nature and causes of rheumatic and other associated disorders and explain the reasons for failure of certain widely practised medical treatments.

It must be understood that there is no *single* cause of rheumatic diseases and thus no single remedy. Unless this is borne in mind the reader may fail to realise that what goes on in the stomach and intestine, for example, may later have a direct bearing on his or her rheumatic or arthritic condition. Thus the reader will find that the early chapters of this book are devoted to explanations of the various processes involved in the workings of the body and the necessity of integrating these processes in our attempts to restore health and rebuild damaged tissues, all of which is essential in the treatment of rheumatic conditions.

The lack of success of medical researches stems from failure to accept that these diseases involve the *whole person,* and not merely isolated muscles and joints and that, therefore, 'whole person' treatment is required, including certain measures of self-help.

Equally important, this book will make quite clear the why and wherefore, the purpose and expected outcome of each and every form of treatment described in succeeding chapters. In this way it should enable the reader to realise that only by relating cause to effect and taking steps to eliminate both may we expect to enable the body's intrinsic natural healing efforts to succeed in restoring and maintaining positive health.

These are the direct paths to health which have already been successfully followed by many thousands of sufferers who, as a result, have experienced a new joy of living.

Contents

List of Illustrations

Part One

Causes and Effects

CHAPTER 1

Arthritis, a Major Problem

The burdens imposed upon the resources of modern civilisation by the incidence of rheumatic diseases are not confined to the many sufferers directly concerned. These burdens concern us all to an extent that is seldom fully realised.

If asked to name the most prevalent type of disease in Britain at the present time it is probable that most people would say 'rheumatism', and they would be right. Those who are most likely to be interested in reading this book, chief among whom may be sufferers from one or other of the many forms of rheumatic ailments, will find no difficulty in accepting this estimate of the widespread incidence of these distressing conditions.

Confirmation of this state of affairs appeared in the form of a report issued by the Arthritis and Rheumatism Council for Research which stated: 'Rheumatism is Britain's most widespread disease. More people have it at any one time than any other ailment.'

The report also stated: 'Only one person in fifty will escape some form of rheumatic disease by the time they reach the age of 70.'

Startling as the above figures appear to be, if the total impact of rheumatic disease upon our modern civilised community is to be fully assessed, much more than just the number of cases seeking medical aid must be taken into account. First, it should be realised that a great number of the earlier or less severe signs of incipient rheumatism tend to come and go, perhaps easing spontaneously time after time as they recur. This pattern of experience may occur to some extent with a number of other complaints also. Frequently, milder attacks are self-medicated with aspirin or other 'household remedies', which are taken so freely for sundry aches, pains and twinges, the causes of which may be attributed to factors such as muscle strain or to having been in a draught or perhaps just to the weather. Many millions of pounds are spent annually on such remedies purchased without medical prescription and so such cases are not included in medical statistics.

Also, in many cases the presence of rheumatism may be masked by some other illness which may appear to be more urgent and perhaps more dangerous, the doctor having been consulted for this other illness. Rheumatism is not regarded as being a killer disease and thus it often does not have first claim on a doctor's attention, especially in its milder forms and earlier stages. In this way also very many cases of rheumatism do not appear in the medical statistics. Therefore, although it is said that about five million people suffering from one or other of the rheumatic diseases consult their doctors annually in England and Wales, this figure may be regarded as being merely the tip of the iceberg when considering the total burden of rheumatic complaints. Moreover, this burden is not confined to the sufferers only; it affects many others in numerous ways and has a considerable impact upon the general community.

First, there are several ways in which others may be affected – husband or wife, son or daughter and sometimes close friends – who may be involved from a sense of sympathy or duty towards a severely affected arthritic, suffering in many cases extra burdens, restrictions and anxieties due to the sufferer's distress and disability.

In addition to such personal problems there are other great social and economic aspects of the burden imposed upon society by the prevalence of rheumatic diseases. The monetary cost to the community has never been fully estimated. The Industrial Survey Unit of the Arthritis and Rheumatism Council issued a report after ten years' research which estimated that some 37 million working days annually are lost, costing more than £200 million in lost wages each year to the sufferers and much more to their employers in lost production and disruption. In this estimate again the figures are conservative, as they are based on medical certification of absences which apply only to absences above four days. It is admitted that there are millions more cases of absence for one, two or three days because of rheumatism which are not recorded.

To this must be added the cost of treatment of rheumatic ailments to the National Health Service. This must be an appreciable proportion of the total costs of the NHS which were approaching £7,000 million in 1978. In addition to the cost of drugs there is the cost of physiotherapy, of surgery and a considerable amount of doctors' time, both general practitioners and consultants.

At this point the reader suffering from rheumatism may feel that, as far as statistics are concerned, this does not appear to help him to find a solution to his personal problem. On the contrary, quite under-standably, he may feel that the very magnitude of the figures for the incidence of these diseases condemns him to continued, perhaps increasing, pain and disability. His experience of medical aid may have reinforced this despondency in that he has already realised that not any of the many pills, tablets, injections or any other form of drug

4

treatment prescribed by his doctor can afford a permanent cure for his complaint.

Meanwhile very many antirheumatic drugs have been issued from the drug houses year by year – many to be discarded either because of ineffectiveness or due to dangerous and damaging side-effects. In the event, aspirin – the oldest of all – is still widely used in spite of its dangerous side-effects.

The reader will have discovered – indeed, in answer to his questions his medical adviser may have admitted the truth – that at best drug treatments give no more than temporary relief of one symptom or another.

Scientific Medicine

In this situation it may be unfair to blame the doctor, who is merely pursuing the conventional practice of so-called scientific medicine. In this way, with the best will in the world the general practitioner can do no more, and even from the best of consultant rheumatologists the patient may get no more satisfaction even though he may be given the latest product of a drug manufacturer, which may well be the least well tested because it is the newest.

Sooner or later, in the course of this process the patient is almost certain to be told that he must 'learn to live with his complaint' and may find that he is faced with an endless vista of medication with drugs which at best mask the aches and pains but almost certainly will produce side-effects which often appear to be worse than the disease for which the drug is prescribed. If his rheumatic condition results in the destructive processes which are characteristic of arthritis this may reach the stage where the patient is offered surgery.

Why No Cure?

In such a situation the patient may be expected to feel a deep sense of frustration and to wonder why the medical profession is unable to produce a cure for rheumatism.

For more than half a century, year after year, substantial sums have been spent in researches in the field of rheumatic diseases, researches which are still continuing with increasing expenditure (recently of the order of £700,000 annually) with the result that no specific cure for arthritis and other rheumatic diseases has been produced.

Modern science has produced many startling results in a number of areas other than medicine. Men have been sent to the moon, and the potential for the destruction of whole populations at the touch of a button has been achieved, but in the same space of time researches in the field of arthritis and rheumatism have been no more successful than the parallel researches for a cure for the common cold. Both of these diseases are still with us in a big way. Also, the appeals continue for more money to finance more and more research with the oft-repeated hopeful suggestion that if more money is forthcoming a 'breakthrough' may appear. All that has appeared so far has been more ineffective drugs to add to the ever-lengthening list.

It may well be wondered why this elusive 'breakthrough' (a somewhat dramatic word – perhaps more applicable to such events as bank raids or underground rescue operations) has failed to appear. There are, in fact, very good reasons for this which will be considered in a later chapter. Meanwhile, the sufferer from arthritis or other form of rheumatism is left with the doctor's proposal that he 'learn to live with it' and continue taking the tablets.

Fortunately, for most of those suffering from arthritis and rheumatism there is no need to abandon hope of a cure in the majority of cases and of very substantial improvement in others. There are well tested and successful methods of treating these conditions which offer a valid and, indeed, a much superior alternative to the treatments of so-called modern scientific medicine.

In using the word 'cure' it is not suggested that some specific, magical pill, tablet, injection or drug of any sort exists which in itself may be termed a 'cure' for any of the conditions with which this book is concerned. The methods of natural therapy specified and explained in the following chapters are derived from an understanding of the nature and causes of these complaints and in accordance with the basic laws of health and disease. Accordingly, the methods of treatment are founded upon the same principles of which they are a practical application.

Whereas with modern orthodox medicine patients are seldom, if ever, required or encouraged to understand and take an interest in the whys and wherefores of the use of drugs and other medical treatments, in the case of the methods of natural therapy, even though it may be possible to apply these methods purely by rule of thumb, it is highly desirable and very helpful to gain some understanding of the principles and practice involved. Such an understanding will clearly indicate the value and necessity of intelligent co-operation of the person concerned if the best possible results are to be obtained.

Not Only the Elderly

The following chapters are intended to supply this information in

6

terms which are simple, clear and explicit, but without requiring any involved technical or scientific expertise in order to understand the nature and purpose of the treatments and so to carry out whatever measures of self-help are necessary in order to secure the most satisfactory results.

It is widely supposed that rheumatic troubles, including arthritis, are diseases of the elderly. This idea may be fostered by the doctors who tell all but the younger patients that 'it's your age' (as if that would explain all) and usually suggest that they 'should learn to live with it', but rheumatic disorders are very common in younger persons, including early childhood. Some of these cases may be serious, but there are many others in which discomforts and pains are commonly dismissed (usually wrongly) as 'only growing-pains'.

CHAPTER 2

A Disease of Many Forms

Medical terminology may be confusing to the non-medical or lay reader. A brief description of the principal forms of rheumatic ailments may help towards better understanding. It will be noted that the suffix '–itis', meaning inflammation, occurs in almost every instance.

The word *rheumatism* has ancient origins, being based upon the idea that the disease conditions to which it applied were associated with watery deposits in the joints. But nowadays the term *rheumatism* includes a wide range of complaints the extent of which is much greater and more diverse than most people may realise.

The many different names given to rheumatic complaints are in the main related to the specific tissues which are involved. In some cases also the names relate to differences in symptoms and to the course of resulting degenerative processes. All these have in common that they are inflammatory conditions which sooner or later result in producing greater or lesser degrees of degenerative changes in the affected tissues. In dealing with rheumatic diseases the medical literature consistently asserts that the causes of rheumatism are unknown, and in consequence medical writers state that this makes classification difficult. Furthermore, as already mentioned, it is admitted by the medical profession that a cure for rheumatism has not yet been found – an admission which generally leads to failure of treatment and further pleas for more large sums of money for medical research.

It is intended in this book to show that both of the above assertions concerning causation and treatment are fallacious and, furthermore, to present a logical basis of understanding of rheumatic diseases and also the corresponding methods of treatment, the value of which has already been well proven, and which are immediately available to all who now suffer from arthritis and other rheumatic complaints.

To many readers these statements may appear to be incredible. 'Surely', they may say, 'modern scientific research has solved very many problems, and so it should be only a matter of ample funds for persistent research to discover both the causes and the cure by modern scientific methods in the field of arthritis and all the other forms of rheumatic disease.'

This view, which in the main represents the present orthodox approach, has proved notably unsuccessful and, while in one sense it is an oversimplification, it has in its therapeutic application produced ever-increasing complications. To say the least, the reality is very different and therefore, in order to understand the reasons for this divergence of outlook, it is of the utmost importance to consider a number of relevant facts which will serve to clarify the issue as regards rheumatic ailments and the need to illuminate many obscurities in the whole field of health and disease.

Thus it will be helpful to consider first the many terms under which corresponding forms of rheumatic disease are classified and described. Incidentally, some of the following ailments might not be recognised by some readers as belonging to the category of rheumatic diseases.

In this classification the main division distinguishes between those rheumatic conditions which affect the soft tissues such as muscles, ligaments, tendons, sheaths, etc. and those conditions which affect bones and joints and are classified as *arthritic* diseases. This is a convenient though not rigid distinction, because in many cases both soft tissues and joints are involved. A considerable number of terms are used to describe the various manifestations of soft-tissue rheumatism.

Soft-Tissue Disorders

The term *muscular rheumatism (myositis)* has now been largely superseded by the term *fibrositis* which literally means inflammation of fibrous tissue, thus including the white fibrous connective tissues which pervade all regions of the body and form a supporting framework for various organs, loosely connecting muscle to muscle and skin to the underlying muscles. This tissue forms the covering sheaths of muscles, nerves and other organs, being widely distributed as sheets and bands of tissue and including tendons to form muscle attachments and ligaments between bones. The joint ligaments linking bone to bone are sufficiently loose to allow normal joint movement while at the same time checking excessive movement and acting in a protective capacity.

Panniculitis is the name given to a form of fibrositis, often painful, under the skin in fatty tissue sites such as the thighs, buttocks, the back of the lower neck and between the shoulders, mainly in those who are overweight. The affected tissues become lumpy and may be slightly dimpled, an effect that is most marked in the thighs and buttocks.

Neuritis is the term applied to inflammatory, painful conditions of specific nerves and their sheaths. Such conditions affecting the shoulder and arm may be called *brachial neuritis*; if situated in the muscles between the ribs the term *intercostal neuritis* may be used; and if affecting the sciatic nerve – the largest nerve in the body – it will be named *sciatica*. Such conditions may be extremely painful.

Synovitis means inflammation of the membrane lining a joint in which there is an increased secretion of synovial fluid, which normally provides for the very efficient lubrication of joints. If persistent, this may be the prelude to the onset of arthritis in the joint concerned; it is commonly found in the knee-joints. The term *capsulitis* is used for a similar condition.

Tenosynovitis is a rheumatic inflammatory condition involving tendons and their sheaths.

Bursitis is the term applied to painful inflammation and enlargement of a *bursa*. The bursae are pouches of fibrous tissue lined with synovial membrane and containing some fluid.

They are situated at points where there is much pressure or friction, such as where one muscle rubs against another or against a bone. Such sites include the shoulder-joint, the elbow and the heel (beneath the achilles tendon). There are several bursae around the knee-joint, and the condition popularly termed 'housemaid's knee' is an inflammation and enlargement of the patellar bursa in the front of the knee immediately below the kneecap.

Lumbago is perhaps the most medically nondescript term in the list of rheumatic disorders. It literally means pain in the lumbar region and usually indicates a rheumatic condition confined to the soft tissues, in its earlier stages, but later the underlying joints may become involved. The causes of such low-back pain must be distinguished from referred pain caused by abdominal and pelvic conditions as against a purely rheumatic disorder.

The conditions of *'frozen shoulder'* and *'tennis elbow'* are basically rheumatic disorders.

The above list includes most forms of soft-tissue rheumatism. Although a useful classification, it must be appreciated that the distinction between these disorders and the various conditions of joint rheumatism termed *arthritis* is not as clear-cut as might be imagined. In all conditions of arthritis it is almost certain that changes in the associated soft tissues are also involved. In particular, injuries to joints are almost invariably associated with inflammatory or degenerative changes in the closely related soft tissues. Conversely, long-standing soft-tissue rheumatic conditions are likely to result in arthritic disease in the underlying joints.

Arthritis is the heading under which the following terms are used to describe the main forms of joint disease. The main distinction is between *osteoarthritis* and *rheumatoid arthritis*.

Osteoarthritis is the term used to describe degenerative conditions mainly concerning the heavy-duty and weight-bearing joints such as the knees, hips, and shoulders, in any of which cartilage may become roughened and possibly worn away, so that eventually bony erosion may take place at the weight-bearing surfaces. Calcium deposits may form steadily around the joint margins, producing spurs and lipping of the joints.

These outgrowths are called *osteophytes*. While calcium salts, which are responsible for the hardness in bones, are thus being deposited; in other areas calcium may be absorbed from the bones, causing weakening and further erosion of bone.

Similar osteoarthritic processes in the spine are termed *spondylitis* (or *spondylosis* when the later, degenerative, changes have taken place). When the joints on either side of the *sacrum* – the large triangular bone at the base of the spine – which articulate with the corresponding side of the pelvis to form the *sacroiliac* joints are similarly affected, the inflammatory stage is known as *sacroiliitis*.

Corresponding arthritic processes in the bones of the neck are referred to as *cervical spondylitis*.

Traumatic arthritis is the term given to the secondary results which may follow an accident or other form of injury or severe strain. It is frequently a later development of the effects of falls, severe sprains and other injuries. Frequently, it develops as a sequel to road accidents, even after the patient has been discharged from hospital with the report, 'No bone injury'. Traumatic arthritis may sometimes develop long after accidents in sports of the more violent and dangerous types. This would largely account for the fact that arthritic hip and other rheumatic joint conditions are found more commonly in middle-aged males than in females.

Rheumatoid arthritis originates as an acute disease which may eventually develop into a chronic condition. It presents characteristic signs and symptoms which distinguish it from osteoarthritis.

Two other conditions which have their own characteristic symptoms are:

Ankylosing spondylitis (ankylosis = locking) in which, as the name suggests – following an acute or chronic inflammation – spinal joints stiffen and eventually lock. The end-result may produce a rigid spine which has been termed 'poker-back'. Its onset occurs usually in the late

11

teens or in the twenties and it is ten times more frequent in males than in females.

Gout, a condition which was common up to four or five decades ago, after which it declined, but recently it has been on the increase again. It occurs in the extremities, and a typical attack is characterised by a sudden severe pain in a big toe and sometimes in other toes. It may occur in the fingers and other joints such as the feet, ankles, wrists or possibly the knees.

Acute Rheumatism (rheumatic fever)

In the study of rheumatic diseases the acute form is particularly significant. It is a disorder of the general system with much pain in joints, which become inflamed. It occurs mainly in children and young adults, with the temperature rising to 102° or 103° F and in some cases even higher. The prevalence of the acute form of rheumatic fever was very high in the early part of this century, since when it has decreased considerably. It is estimated that there are now about 20,000 cases per annum. The heart is liable to be affected in rheumatic fever, and it is estimated that 'there are about 200,000 people with rheumatic heart disease now in Great Britain and that 11 million people have had rheumatic fever' (report from the Office of Health Economics).

The present situation is that the very acute form of rheumatic fever with high temperature has become uncommon and that a *subacute rheumatism* is more usual. This does not mean that damage to heart, joints, etc., is necessarily avoided.

This brief list and description of rheumatic complaints indicates the widespread nature of these ailments. Also, it may enable many of those whose medical diagnosis has been expressed in one or other of the above terms to appreciate the nature of their trouble. This, in itself, may help to disperse fears of the unknown, particularly if, as in this book, it is related to possible treatment which, in contrast with the mere suppression or relief of symptoms with drugs, is in turn related to the natural causes of the disease. The methods of treatment to be described have already proved successful in very many thousands of cases.

CHAPTER 3

Vital Questions

The symptoms of rheumatism and arthritis may cause much distress to the sufferer, but are these manifestations of the disease itself and how are they related to the real causes of the disease? The choice of treatment will depend mainly on finding the right answers to these and other relevant questions.

At this point readers may have formulated a number of questions.

First, it may be asked why such difficulty seems to exist in ascertaining the causes of rheumatism. To a great extent the reason for this lack of success in the realm of medical research is that doctors are looking primarily to the laboratories, including those of the manufacturing chemists – the drug houses – to find the much-needed solution of this very urgent, vitally important problem.

The Concept of Chemotherapy

Throughout the present century researches into the causes and treatment of diseases have been directed mainly in accordance with the concept of *chemotherapy.* This word means literally 'treatment by chemicals', and it was first developed by a German physician, Paul Ehrlich (1854–1915), on the basis of the germ theory of disease causation. The definition of *chemotherapy* is given as 'the treatment of disease by administering chemicals which affect the causative organism unfavourably but do not injure the patient'. Ehrlich spent most of his life searching for such specific chemicals. These remedies, which Ehrlich was convinced should exist, were somewhat romantically referred to as 'magic bullets'.

Added impetus was given to these searches by the simultaneous development of synthetic chemistry, which offered an ever-increasing and never-ending multitude of compounds, most of which have never existed in the realm of nature. They were, and still are, selected and promoted on the basis of a limited number of experiments on animals and ultimately on humans.

The ideal 'magic bullets' have never been found, but it is upon such lines that medical research has mainly proceeded and is still proceeding. In the case of rheumatism, as with many other diseases, the search for a specific micro-organism has been unsuccessful. No germ, bacterium or virus that might be regarded as the cause of rheumatism has ever been identified among the vast multitude of germs which are ever with us on our skin, in the respiratory tract, the alimentary tract and elsewhere in our environment, both internal and external. Most people may not realise that it is an indisputable fact that most of these germs, far from harming us, are not merely tolerated but are helpful to the extent that they are indispensable to our continued good health. Under normal conditions, our natural germ colonies are self-regulating so as to preserve a state of balance among the many and varied indigenous (i.e. normally present) micro-organisms, a condition termed *symbiosis*.

What are the Germs doing?

Not only are the indigenous microbes consistent with a state of good health but many of them perform beneficial functions which are necessary to safeguard our health. In particular, the bacterial colonies in our gastro-intestinal tract play a very important part in the processes of digestion and, what is more, are stated to produce certain valuable amino-acids and also a number – at least six – of essential vitamins. Thus our intestine may be regarded as a busy workshop for the conversion of food to nutrition.

It has been considered that the *streptococcus* bacterium might be the cause of rheumatism because, although it is a normal constituent of intestinal flora, it may appear in other sites in the body in rheumatic fever.

However, it is also present in a number of other septic and feverish conditions but it is not claimed to be the cause of those conditions. It is said that these bacteria are *'found in association* with these conditions', which is quite different from saying that they are the direct *cause* of the conditions.

In situations where there exists a well balanced relationship between living organisms, humans, animals, micro-organisms and plants, etc., so that the association is beneficial to one or both, this harmonious state, as already mentioned, is known as *symbiosis,* the word literally meaning 'living together'. These symbiotic systems are very important in the study of natural, living organisms, and in evaluating problems of health and disease in particular, but up to the present their study has been greatly neglected.

It may also be asked whether rheumatism may be caused by a virus. Nowadays, the ubiquitous virus is blamed for a large proportion of common and uncommon illnesses, but its role is not as simple as it might seem. In the course of the long-term, painstaking researches which have been carried out in the hope of finding a cause of the common cold, the presence of many types of viruses has been demonstrated but neither a particular bacterium nor a single virus has been identified as being the specific cause of the common cold.

The only possible conclusion from these researches is that there appears to be no single cause of the common cold and thus there is still no cure, no 'magic bullet', to knock out this tiresome complaint. Similarly, in spite of a century of medical research, no specific rheumatic germ, bacterium or virus has been identified and no 'magic bullet' – drug, injection or other chemical treatment – has emerged as a cure for rheumatism.

Is it therefore possible that research scientists have been so occupied in looking down their microscopes and ultramicroscopes that they have failed to observe and to evaluate quite different factors in the cause, development and progress of these illnesses?

Rheumatics in the Sun

Another question arises from the notion that climatic conditions, particularly changeable, damp and cold climates, are a cause of rheumatism. Certainly there are many sufferers who claim to be able to forecast such weather changes by variations in their rheumatic pains, and, indeed, in order to find an answer to this question a medical investigation into the incidence of arthritis in Jamaica, a region noted for its equable climate, was carried out. A report on the results of this investigation was issued in 1967 and showed clearly that, in spite of the favourable climate, the Jamaicans had almost the same amount of arthritis as the population of Great Britain. It was, however, felt less severely in terms of pain in Jamaica, the symptoms being less severe to the extent that relatively little working time was lost.

It was concluded that in the warm, dry climate of Jamaica the *pain threshold* was higher. The report stated, 'It would seem that Granny is right when she says that she can tell when it is going to rain by an increase in her rheumatic pains.' The only positive recommendation made was that 'in Britain where about 30 million working days a year are lost through rheumatic complaints employers might be able to reduce this total by providing a drier, warmer atmosphere at work'.

The implementation of this suggestion would not, however, be likely to reduce the incidence of rheumatism. Hot, dry atmospheres at work are already not uncommon and any attempt to effect an increase might serve only to add to the discomforts due to the drastic atmospheric changes on entering and leaving workplaces.

With regard to the existence of a *threshold of pain,* it is important to understand the nature and significance of this phenomenon, which will be considered in a later chapter.

A further question may be asked, namely, whether rheumatic ailments are universal. Do all nations and races suffer in a similar way and to a similar extent from painful, inhibiting and often crippling rheumatic conditions? The answer is that from one human community to another there are major differences in the patterns and incidence of disease and the experience of health, not least in the case of rheumatic diseases. The examination of the possible reasons for such variations has revealed a number of indications which have proved to be very helpful towards the understanding of possible causes of rheumatism and the solution of a number of problems relating to the disease in its many forms.

Concerning the all-important question of whether all forms of rheumatism, particularly arthritis, are incurable – as so many sufferers have been told by their medical advisers – it is quite true that there is no single medicine of any kind which may be claimed to be a cure for any of these rheumatic disorders.

It may well be asked why medical treatment is so unsatisfactory. Why has the long-hoped-for breakthrough not been achieved? It may well be that orthodox medicine is striving for the impossible. In order to find acceptable answers to these and other questions it is necessary to realise that both health and disease are subject to natural laws, and that effects are always related to causes. It should also be realised that the idea of 'fighting' nature is a false, dangerous and misleading concept in regard to the realities of health and disease. Rather should we endeavour to understand the basic principles which govern health and disease in order that we may relate them at every stage if we are to find safe and effective methods of treating rheumatism, and conceivably many other diseases also.

Bearing in mind these essential requirements, it is necessary to explain some of the fallacious and irrational ideas which bedevil modern medical science and which largely explain its limitations, dangers and failures.

Moreover, many people find it hard to accept that there is a viable alternative to the practice of chemotherapy, even after having experienced disappointment under orthodox treatment. More questions and doubts may arise from the fact that the natural alternative is practised mainly outside the medical orbit.

Advocates of natural therapy are repeatedly faced with questions such as 'Why do the doctors not recognise you?' and 'Why are these

16

methods not available on the National Health Service?' or 'My doctor has sent me to a specialist who has said there is no cure for my trouble. Can he possibly be mistaken?' These and other similar questions add to the doubts and confusions which deter so many sufferers when an alternative course is suggested. In this situation, explanation and instruction are very necessary if misunderstandings are to be resolved.

CHAPTER 4

The Doctors' Dilemma
1: The Heritage

Nowadays the drugs used by the medical profession have changed but many of the ancient fallacies still persist to dominate and often to confuse the medical scene.

In the introduction to his book *Need Your Doctor Be So Useless?*, Dr Andrew Malleson, a scientific officer of the Medical Research Council, states:

Doctors deal with disease, sometimes competently but often not. Their profession is the child of the barber surgeons and the quack magicians whose traditions die hard . . . Health, or rather ill health, is vote catching, and politicians legislate for it. Ill health is big business, doctors and many others make their living by it, and pharmaceutical firms their fortunes . . . Hippocrates, the Father of Medicine, taught that doctors should above all things be useful to their patients, and should do them no harm.

These comments by Dr Malleson exemplify the quandary in which the medical profession finds itself – a quandary the like of which has not been experienced by any other learned profession. Certain aspects of modern medicine can be better understood if it is realised how and why this unique situation has arisen. It will also help to explain many of the admitted inadequacies and failures in the treatment of many of our most common problems of health and disease.

It is not only as regards rheumatism – the most prevalent of our diseases – that the doctor has to admit that in spite of all the vast sums spent on research, paid for largely from public funds and charitable contributions, the specific causes are still unknown. The same verdict applies to many other forms of illness and particularly the chronic, degenerative diseases which are responsible for the major part of modern ill health, and for most of which no specific 'cure' has been discovered.

18

Growing Dissatisfaction

Among the lay public there appears to be a growing sense of dissatisfaction concerning medical services, and the reasons for this state of affairs certainly appear to be valid. Despite this trend, however, the great majority of people still seek the doctors' services for their many and varied complaints so that the surgeries for the most part are overcrowded and the doctor has little time available for the average patient. Those suffering from rheumatic troubles, as with other chronic diseases, are likely to be told, sooner or later, that there is no cure for these conditions and they will be advised that they should 'learn to live with it', while drugs will be prescribed in the hope of easing the more distressing symptoms, often without any pretence that the medicine may cure the disease.

It seems that the majority of doctors today do not envisage any possible alternative; nevertheless a valid alternative *does* exist, although the majority of doctors regard it as being of little or no importance and as yet it is not sufficiently well known to, and understood by, the general public.

To gain some understanding as to why and how orthodox medicine has arrived at this virtual impasse, and before attempting to explain and describe the natural alternative, a brief, factual explanation is called for, concerning the events in medical history which have led to the present anomalous and irrational system in which 'modern scientific medicine' finds itself.

The idea of miraculous cures dates from the dawn of medical history. In ancient Egypt, India, Greece and elsewhere magical remedies, often grotesque, were many and varied, and usually seemingly irrational. Eventually, in Greece, from about 1000 BC onwards, signs of a rational, scientific outlook began to appear, culminating in the great teachings of Hippocrates (born 460 BC on the island of Cos), which were recorded and handed down to posterity. Hippocrates became known as the 'Father of Medicine', and his sayings are still quoted in the university lectures of professors of medicine all over the world.

The Father of Medicine

Hippocrates rejected the 'demon theory' which was held at the time and asserted that disease was due to natural causes and that therefore the physician's duty towards his patient was to observe, examine and so to deduce such causes. From this he proceeded to develop diagnosis and from that to establish prognosis – the forecasting of the prospect of recovery – as never before.

19

Beyond that, he stated that 'our natures are the physicians of our diseases' and furthermore asserted that medical skill and treatment at its best would never be more than a supplement to the healing power of nature. He further stipulated that the aim of the physician in his efforts to help the natural healing process must be 'at least to do no harm'.

The Hippocratic oath which he required his pupils to take is theoretically still in line with the modern code of medical ethics.

Hippocrates was strongly opposed to the use of drugs, which he considered to be harmful, and he himself used very few medicines and those mainly simple, non-poisonous herbs. He attached great importance to diet and to necessary rest, and prominent among his treatments was the use of water in the form of baths, fomentations and poultices. He also used some forms of manipulative treatment, and understood the value of fasting in cases of fever and other illnesses.

In the time of Hippocrates, the clinics were the Greek temples where, in a helpful environment of beauty and peace, the natural treatments which he favoured would be effectively employed.

A further important principle recognised by Hippocrates was that many of the symptoms which he observed in disease were evidence of the body's natural curative reactions, and that, as such, they should be assisted towards the attainment of their objective. This was expressed by Hippocrates in the saying 'Give me a fever, and I can cure your patient.'

Hippocrates used surgery where he considered it necessary to deal with injuries, to set fractures, reduce dislocations, to drain pus and certain other emergencies. He gave strict instructions for cleanliness in surgery thus anticipating the modern principle of asepsis. In this, he was undoubtedly ahead of the medical practices of the nineteenth century AD, when at last Semmelweis, the physician of Vienna, fought for improved standards of cleanliness and antisepsis in 1847.

No doubt the Hippocratic school of medicine contributed to the physical excellence for which the ancient Greeks have been renowned.

Unfortunately, the later Greek physicians failed to adhere to the strict principles and practice of the Hippocratic school, the chief reason being the increasing return to the use of drugs.

Over three hundred years later Galen, the leading doctor of his time, professed complete faith in the healing power of nature, but nevertheless he used drugs far more extensively than Hippocrates had advised.

During the long period of the dark ages and the medieval centuries the Arabic schools of chemistry and medicine flourished for a thousand years up to the time of the Renaissance. Under their influence the pharmacopoeia, the list of drugs ('drug' was an Arabic

20

word), was greatly increased. Many drugs were known to be poisonous, but were not struck off the list unless they were judged to be too obviously lethal.

In Christendom, for many centuries the care of the sick was almost entirely in the hands of the monks, who viewed disease as a punishment for sin, and treatment was mainly confined to care and comfort of the suffering.

The English Hippocrates

In the thirteenth century, medicine passed from the monk once again to the physician and it was re-established as a profession; it was then that the word 'doctor' was first used for physicians. From the thirteenth century onwards a number of medical schools were established but, although throughout these years the translated works of Hippocrates and his followers were taught, his methods of treatment were generally neglected. Meanwhile, the lengthy drug lists of the pharmacopoeia remained in constant use as the main therapeutic armament of the physician, even though from time to time certain of the wiser doctors – such as Paracelsus in the sixteenth century and, in the seventeenth century, Thomas Sydenham, who became known as the 'English Hippocrates' by virtue of his return to the teaching and much of the practice of the great Greek physician – deplored the overuse of drugs. This reform was much needed at this time in view of the general medical treatment with overdosage of drugs which were mainly useless and all too often harmful while more rational methods were neglected.

Sydenham had read the works of Hippocrates and declared them to have 'arrived at the highest pitch of physick'. Like Hippocrates, he realised that all diseases had natural origins and so endeavoured to assist the body's healing by simple means, following the Hippocratic rule that a healer should 'do good, or at least do no harm', from which he verified that 'nature alone terminates distempers . . . sometimes without any medicines at all'.

As might be expected, such views shocked both his colleagues and his patients and produced considerable opposition. In the event, this call to a return to Hippocratic principles did little or nothing to stem the torrent of drugs poured into the long-suffering sick.

Henry VIII and the Doctors

The physicians, elevated far above the surgeons and bone setters, established control of drugs (the Charter of the Royal College of

21

Physicians was granted by Henry VIII in 1518).

Before 1745 surgery was practised largely by barber-surgeons, who were considered to be tradesmen and treated with contempt. The teachings of Sydenham appear to have been largely disregarded. In the later eighteenth century the use of drugs in large dosages reached a drastic crisis under the leadership of John Brown (1735–88), whose theories were termed the Brunonian system. In Britain John Brown and in France Broussais were said to have 'caused more deaths than the French Revolution and the Napoleonic Wars combined'.

The torrent of drugs continued to flow throughout the eighteenth century and in fact the physicians became a force in society as never before. An average physician's income was about £5,000 a year (equivalent to at least £70,000 or £80,000 in our present time). All this professional wealth and status was built upon the gullibility of society perpetuated by means of the 'mystique' of the 'magical drug'.

The idea of specialisation developed from the second half of the eighteenth century and with it came a further elevation of the physician's status and wealth. Although, during the eighteenth century, the teachings of Sydenham appear to have been largely disregarded, medical history records an eighteenth century exception in this respect in the person of the Dutch physician, Hermann Boerhaave of the University of Leiden, who became known as the 'Batavian Hippocrates'. With a small hospital of only twelve beds it is recorded that this great teacher, known for his gentleness and kindness as well as for the fame of his teaching, attracted pupils 'from Edinburgh to Vienna'. It was said that he was 'probably the finest clinical teacher of the eighteenth century; he brought the wisdom of Hippocrates to the lecture room and encouraged his pupils to observe living patients as well as to study skeletons'. His pupil, Van Sweiten, reorganised the medical school of Vienna so that it eventually became one of the leading medical centres in Europe.

Later in the eighteenth century the German doctor Samuel Hahnemann experimented with the drugs of his day but using smaller doses. In view of the massive dosages of highly poisonous drugs that were being prescribed at that time it was fully understandable that more of his patients survived and made a natural recovery. Hahnemann proceeded further and found that even smaller doses gave still better results and he explained this by postulating that the smaller the dosage of a drug which, in large doses, caused similar symptoms, the more 'potent' was its effect. According to his theory, the more infinitesimally small were the doses, the more potent were their curative effects. Hahnemann also paid considerable attention to the role of nutrition in illness. At least his treatments were in

22

accordance with the Hippocratic aphorism, 'at least to do no harm'.

Taking the Waters

The same assurance concerning safety of treatment applied in the case of water treatments (hydrotherapy), which became very widely used and very popular during the eighteenth and nineteenth centuries. After a lapse of many centuries, the Roman baths at Bath became once again a popular venue for eighteenth century society and many other spas followed suit, in Britain and many parts of Europe.

Apart from the well-known spas, then mainly used by the wealthy, a number of pioneers of nature cure established centres where patients were treated with dietary, fasting, hydrotherapy and other natural treatments. One of the first of these was Arnold Rikli, who established a 'Light and Air' sanatorium in Austria. Others who were providing similar treatments included Vincent Priessnitz who, instead of relying on the heavy drugging of that time, used well devised hydrotherapy combined with a simple dietary of fresh foods, fresh air and exercise. His methods had much success and his fame spread far and wide.

Another successful pioneer of hydrotherapy and other natural treatments was Johannes Schroth, also of Austria, while Louis Kunhe, in Germany, studied natural methods for a number of years before opening a nature cure establishment in Leipzig.

He wrote a number of books on the subject, one of the best-known being entitled *The New Science of Healing*.

Another German, Adolphe Just, founded a sanatorium in the Harz mountains, and in his book *Return to Nature* he described how the whole body can be renewed or rejuvenated by natural living, claiming that disease is the consequence of the violation of nature's laws. Sebastian Kneipp, in Bavaria, carried on a busy clinic for more than forty-five years until his decease in 1897, using dietary treatments, hydrotherapy and simple herbs.

The successes of these nineteenth-century practitioners, achieved by the use of non-injurious, drugless treatments, resulted in sufferers coming from far and wide to seek treatment, but their work was mainly opposed by the orthodox doctors of the time.

The Germ Theory of Disease

During the nineteenth century great advances were made in physiology, largely due to the development of the microscope, which made possible the observation of the living cells of which the body is composed and which also led to the discovery of the existence of microbes. In the same period there were rapid advances in the field of chemistry.

These advances in turn led to the formulation of the germ theory of disease which was advanced, in the 1860s, by the chemist Louis Pasteur, who postulated that germs (microbes) are the cause of disease and that specific germs were the cause of specific diseases.

As may be imagined, the germ theory was readily seized upon by the medical profession, and its corollary was the search for drugs which could kill the germ without seriously damaging the patient. With the resulting growth of chemical technology, the rapidly developing chemical industry was naturally eager to join in the attack on the ubiquitous microbe. In this regard, as already mentioned, Paul Ehrlich, the German bacteriologist, introduced the concept of *chemotherapy* – the search for a 'magic bullet' for use against each specific germ.

The floodgates were opened, and the ever-increasing torrent of drugs was further swollen with the rapid growth of the chemical industry.

In the nineteenth century, three famous names are linked with new concepts of health and disease. Rudolph Virchow (1821–1902), the German pathologist, postulated that disease is characterised by changes in the living cells. Claude Bernard (1813–98), Professor of Pathology at the Sorbonne University of Paris, emphasised the maintainance of a constant steady state of the vital fluids – blood, tissue fluid and lymph – within narrow limits as an essential condition for life, the tissue fluid being the cell's immediate environment, supplying it with nourishment and oxygen and removing the waste products of metabolism.

Later, in 1929, Professor Walter Cannon of the USA originated the term *homoeostasis* to describe the steady state which must be maintained in the fluids of the body within the required narrow limits. The term *homoeostasis* also applies to the spontaneous reactive processes by which the living body responds to disturbances of this critical balance which may occur from time to time, particularly in disease.

These modern concepts follow Hippocrates' attempts to identify disease with internal as well as external environmental changes. In 1932 Cannon elaborated his views in his classic book *The Wisdom of the Body* and these and other subsequent studies have thrown light on the self-curative power of the body which is evident in so many human ills.

CHAPTER 5

The Doctors' Dilemma
2: Chemotherapy Takes Over

*The twentieth century has seen the years of startling change,
innovation and rapid growth. The modern patterns of disease
are largely the expression of man's failure to adapt to
environmental changes and habits of living. Modern medicine
has endeavoured to develop short cuts of which chemotherapy
and tolerance towards food sophistication are major examples.*

The outstanding characteristic of the twentieth century is one of rapid
change, which has presented human society with great problems of
adaptation, most of all for the inhabitants of those most rapidly
developing countries which are referred to as the 'advanced' nations of
Western civilisation.

The transformations of the last hundred years in engineering,
transport by air, sea and land, and communications by telephone,
radio and television have all stemmed from the developments of the
basic sciences of physics, chemistry and engineering and have
produced changes more vast and significant than those of the whole of
previous recorded history. By no means the least of these innovations
has been the growth of the chemical industries, which have expanded
with great rapidity, producing a vast number of new substances from
paints and plastics to poison sprays and pills. Pre-eminent among
these great modern industries are the multinational, multi-million
cartels known as the 'drug houses'. The resulting impact on the
environment and on medical treatment has greatly modified the
nature and patterns of health and disease. To understand what is
happening in our present society the activities of these very large and
powerful industrial complexes must be evaluated, remembering that
they are in business and so are primarily, and quite naturally,
concerned with profitability. Erlich, if alive today might feel he had
opened a 'Pandora's box'.

Chemicals Galore

Undoubtedly, most people are quite unaware of the full implications

25

of the situation as it now exists. First, the enormous sales figures for drugs (those obtained on doctors' prescriptions as well as those bought over the counter, but excluding drugs of addiction obtained illegally) are so huge that they constitute a significant fraction of our total economy, to such a degree that their sudden discontinuance would upset the figure of the gross national product – the GNP so frequently emphasised by economists and politicians – to the extent of precipitating financial ruin on a national or perhaps on an international scale. This is no exaggeration, as the following quotation will indicate. Professor Arnold Klass was appointed chairman in 1971 of a special commission for the Government of Manitoba to study the manufacture and distribution of pharmaceutical drugs. In his book *There's Gold in Them Thar Pills,* Dr Klass states: 'The total turnover of drug sales in 1971 has been estimated conservatively as sixteen billion dollars [a billion is 1,000 million], with the leaders of the pack a Swiss firm, Hoffman La Roche, having a turnover in 1971 of one thousand two hundred and fifty million dollars.' He further states: 'Even number twenty-two in the list, British Beecham, hit a respectable one hundred and forty-two million dollars.'

These figures are such that even for those not greatly impressed by statistics two important questions must arise. First, there is the question 'How has such a gigantic industry come into being?' The second question may be 'What has this to do with rheumatism?' The answer to the latter question will become apparent when the first question is fully answered.

Matters have gone far since the earlier days of this century when, as some still remember, many doctors had their dispensary behind the surgery and made up their own medicines or relied on the local chemist to make up 'the mixture' as instructed. The rapid development of the techniques of synthetic chemistry, whereby atoms and molecules may be linked together in every conceivable pattern, has opened the possibilities of synthesising virtually an infinite number of substances most of which normally have no part in the scheme of nature.

Consequently, research on the part of the manufacturing chemist has developed in the form of large laboratories with teams of chemists producing ever more synthetic substances, each of which may then be tested for possible commercial uses. From among these many substances, most of which may be alien to our environment, tests on laboratory animals may indicate perhaps only one in hundreds as having physiological properties, affecting one or other factor in the animals' vital processes, for example lowering the blood-pressure, reducing sensitivity (pain-killers or sedatives), calming down (tranquillisers), lowering temperature or reducing inflammation, altering heart speed or rhythm, killing germs, etc. Most of these substances are found to be poisonous, some deadly, others less harmful; others have more insidiously harmful effects; while others – in small doses – may appear to be harmless.

These activities constitute a major part of medical research.

Following animal experiments, the next step will be to carry out trials on human volunteers. The number of animal experiments for the testing of drugs, medical products and appliances for 1977 is officially given as approaching 3 million for Great Britain alone. The number world-wide would be vastly greater, which gives some idea of the extent of these experiments. Among the many synthetic substances thus tested, a few are selected as the modern antirheumatic drugs. These will be added to the list which still includes many of the older remedies, of which not one has been claimed to be a cure. Nor, for that matter, has any one of the new drugs proved to be a cure, even though it may give quick relief of some symptom of the disease. Consequently the sufferer may 'feel better' for a short while, but only until the effect wears off and the time comes for the next dose of pill, tablet or capsule, as the case may be. Thus, the charitable appeals for more research funds are still based on the search for a *cure,* often with the hopeful suggestion that a breakthrough may be imminent provided more money is forthcoming. There are very good reasons for believing that the researches for new drugs, on the lines we have described, are never likely to produce *cures* in the real sense of the word, particularly in chronic degenerative diseases of which the rheumatic diseases are a prime example.

The term 'chemotherapy', initially applied to 'germ-killers', may now be expanded to cover the whole range of chemicals flowing in increasing torrents from the pharmaceutical industry. Thus the profound effects of modern drug treatment have resulted in highly significant changes in medical practice both as regards the patients and the community at large. The nature of these changes largely provides the answer to the question 'Why is it that, in spite of these gigantic scientific activities, the incidence of rheumatic diseases is as great if not greater than ever before (as indeed are many other chronic degenerative diseases)?' This constitutes a major problem in Western civilisation. Some further facts will help to clarify the answer to this very urgent question and to indicate the real path to health, which lies in quite another direction.

Today's physician has an overcrowded surgery and, generally, he has little time to spare for the average patient (estimates vary from three to six minutes). In fact this may not be much more than is needed

27

for the doctor to ask a few questions and to write on his prescription pad. The more serious or potentially serious cases may be sent to hospital, where they are more or less out of his hands. Many conscientious doctors are not happy about this situation, and neither are very many patients.

In the great majority of cases the remedy is prescribed according to the symptoms – drugs to ease pain, to suppress anxiety, to relax, to stimulate ('pep pills'), to sedate ('sleeping pills'), to lower blood-pressure and, of course, all too frequently, one or other of the many available antibiotics, and so forth. In general, these effects are purely temporary, bridging the time-gap to the next dose. Most of these prescriptions will be for one or more of the modern drugs produced and promoted by the multimillionaire drug houses.

'Out-of-date Doctors'

There are several factors in this situation which are not generally known. First, as a number of medical writers have pointed out, the knowledge a doctor has gained in the long and arduous training in medical school nowadays will become out of date in from five to ten years, a fact which is largely responsible for the modern doctors' dilemma. Thus, a doctor's knowledge of the drugs he is handling daily, with new products continually appearing, is not likely to come from his medical school. His educators, by whom he is brought up to date, have become the great and powerful drug houses (the small drug manufacturer is now almost non-existent).

As with all industrial organisations, the drug houses are naturally profit-motivated; this is inevitable. Their profits are large – indeed, for many years they have been up to double the average for all other industries. Dr Andrew Malleson, who has been a scientific officer of the Medical Research Council, has stated: 'English drug firms spend £15 million a year advertising their products to doctors. I have not been able to find out how much American drug companies spend, since this information is not readily available. One author quotes this figure as $750 million.' The drug houses seek to justify this level of expenditure by indicating that profits have to cover three fields, namely (1) research, (2) sales promotion, mainly advertising, and (3) the shareholders' dividends (the latter often a poor third).

A major part of drug promotion is in the form of advertising directed to the doctor. This is presented as professional information, but many would be astonished if they inspected the medical journals to see the glossy, 'hard-sell' type of advertising in which professional instruction appears only in the small print. Doctors are probably no

28

more and no less susceptible to high-power advertising than other people. Information on a drug which could be contained in a few lines, or at most in a quarter-page, is frequently set in a two- or even a four-page spread with sensational emotive wording and illustrations in 'glorious Technicolor', and the same advertisement may be repeated in issue after issue. Adverts for non-medical commodities and subjects are seldom seen in these journals. What is more, publishers of eminent medical journals have stated that without this advertising by the pharmaceutical industry they would no longer be economically viable and would have to cease publication.

In addition, a continuous flow of equally high-pressure advertising literature comes through the doctors' letter-boxes, to an extent that has frequently caused the overworked medical recipient to protest.

High-power Advertising

In addition to this high-pressure advertising the drug manufacturers employ travelling salesmen who call to see the doctor at his surgery or home. These salesmen, often referred to as 'detail men' are not medically qualified. They will have been briefed by means of an intensive course on the medical terminology, what the drug is for, and what it is supposed to do for the patient, together with warnings of any known harmful side-effects that have been identified at such an early stage of its introduction.

In addition to promotional pressures on the doctor, the manufacturers – in many cases – ply editors with information concerning the latest 'wonder' drugs as a basis for articles and reports. These and other items appearing in the popular press – especially accounts of surgery with transplants, spare-part surgery and so forth – impress the lay readers with the wonders of modern scientific medicine. In consequence, it is not surprising that doctors sometimes complain that patients ask for and expect to be given the latest remedies even for minor complaints. The doctor, aware of the possibility of harmful side-effects, may be reluctant to prescribe, but there are medico-legal aspects which, should he refuse, might lay him open to a charge of neglecting the case; or otherwise his patient may go to another doctor. If, however, he prescribes and the known side-effects prove to be worse than the natural symptoms, the patient is unlikely to be successful if he lodges a complaint against the doctor.

With the patient probably inheriting the idea of 'pills for everything' from a long line of ancestors, it is not surprising that he or she should expect results from present-day drugs. At best what he or she may *get* is no more than temporary relief. No cures, in the true sense of the word, are ever obtained from drugs, even for rheumatism and arthritis, the simple reason being that although drugs may deal with some of the *effects*, and afford quick but temporary relief, they do not eradicate the causes of disease.

Thus we may see that throughout the centuries, from the earliest beginnings of medicine, drugs and other 'cures' in great number have been introduced and as many times superseded, while the reputation of the physician has been saved almost as frequently by the healing effort of nature, when the remedy of the moment has been credited with the power of cure.

These considerations apply in modern times, as much as they did in the days of Hippocrates.

CHAPTER 6

The Changing Face of Disease

Too often man's efforts to circumvent nature have proved to be among his costliest mistakes. Sensible measures of public health and hygiene virtually eradicated the virulent fevers of the nineteenth century. Now, in the era of symptom-suppressing drugs and other environmental factors the prevailing ills are the chronic degenerative diseases. These facts must be considered if the causes of rheumatic diseases are to be understood, and if rational treatment is to be deduced and developed.

The nineteenth and twentieth centuries differ from earlier periods in being the era of widespread man-made change. Had it been possible to forecast at the beginning of the nineteenth century and perhaps especially at the end of the nineteenth century the nature and magnitude of these changes resulting from intensive scientific research, our ancestors would never have believed that such revolutionary changes could be possible. Unfortunately, not all of these changes have been entirely beneficial.

We now have instant communication via telephone and radio. We can travel at enormous speeds which we take for granted; even travel in space is possible. The awe-inspiring feats of nuclear physics have given man the power to wreak terrible destruction at the press of a button, and nuclear-test explosions in the antipodes can result in increases of radioactivity capable of causing cancer in the farthest regions of the northern hemisphere. An enormous increase of varied manufactured products now makes available a host of amenities, labour-saving devices, comforts, amusements and so forth.

It is therefore appropriate to inquire how far all this has proved to be of real benefit to the populations of those countries in which this new civilisation has made the greatest strides. Above all, what has it done for our health, happiness and well-being? What are the effects in terms of illness or freedom from physical and mental disease? Are we able to assume that, because our civilised environment has been so greatly changed by the application of the more exact sciences of chemistry, physics and engineering, present-day medical science will produce correspondingly beneficial improvements in the quality of life of the individual? Is it reasonable to suppose that the 'war' against disease,

31

with the 'magic bullets' of chemotherapy as its weapons, will result in the elimination of one illness after another, culminating in the total conquest of disease?

The facts of the situation concerning health today give little or no support to such facile assumptions. Most of the questions remain unanswered. With the rapidly spreading influence of Western civilisation, the idea has spread that applied science must be able to solve all problems. Some have referred to science as being the deity of modern times, with research as its votive ritual. Basically, science is a study of the laws of nature. Scientific technology, on the other hand, may appear to have as its aim the defeat or circumvention of natural law – ignoring the fact that nature is apt to hit back in such an unnatural conflict.

In fact there have occurred profound changes in the nature and incidence of civilised disease since the second half of the last century – changes which have been closely related to social and economic conditions during the same period, changes both in the environment in which we live and in our habits of life. We are heirs to these changes, which have led to the patterns of disease at the present time. During this short period the acute infectious diseases have dramatically declined. With the nineteenth-century movement of population from rural to urban areas, the rapid growth of crowded cities was not accompanied by a corresponding increase in sanitation and hygiene.

Environment and Public Health

For many centuries the classic Hippocratic writings on *Airs, Waters and Places* had been the standard work on the possible effects of the environment upon public health. Professor René Dubos, of the Rockefeller Institute, refers in his book *Man Adapting* to this work of Hippocrates, stating, 'His treatise was used as a practical textbook of medicine and was reprinted for this purpose even as late as 1874. Thus, for two thousand years, the physicians under its influence regarded it as law of nature that, just as every country possesses its own plant and animal kingdoms, so it also possesses a characteristic disease kingdom.'

Airs, Waters and Places was not reprinted as a practical guide to physicians after 1874 because the germ theory of disease and the science of nutrition began at that time to undermine its scientific authority.

It may surprise many readers to know that in 1849 the sanitation of London was so bad that the *Morning Chronicle* referred to London as the 'Venice of Drains'. The Thames itself was in a filthy condition.

32

Cesspools had been abolished, and instead sewage was discharged directly into the Thames and its tributaries. In many parts of London drinking water was taken from the common sewer. Not surprisingly, cholera spread far and wide, as did other virulent infective diseases. In addition, periodic shortages of foods caused malnutrition and added to the plight of the town-dweller and lowered his resistance to disease.

Some improvement in this state of affairs was brought about by a Metropolitan Water Act in 1852 but, in spite of this, London water supplies, under the control of a number of private water companies, were suspect until as late as 1902, when the Metropolitan Water Board bought up all the old companies. Thus cholera, typhoid fever and smallpox, the virulent dirt-and-poverty diseases, were eradicated by means of sensible measures of public health aimed at eliminating the basic causes of these killer diseases. Moreover, the records of the incidence of the infective diseases in children are revealing. This is graphically illustrated in Figure 1, from which it is evident that the

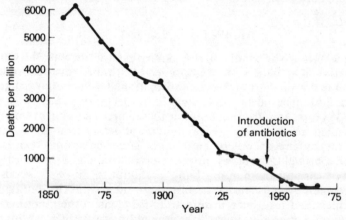

1   Incidence of infective diseases of children

deaths of children under the age of fifteen attributed to scarlet fever, diphtheria, whooping cough and measles were rapidly declining before 1900. The decline continued steadily well before the introduction of antibiotics and the even later introduction of mass immunisation. The only conclusion to be drawn from these statistics is that the introduction of antibiotics and immunisation appears to have

---

[1] *The Contribution of the Biological and Medical Sciences to Human Welfare.* Presidential Addresses of the British Association for Science, 1971. Figure 1 reproduced by courtesy of Professor Porter and of the British Association.

done little or nothing to affect the progressive decline of mortality and morbidity in these childhood infective diseases. Ninety per cent of the reduction had occurred *before* the introduction of these medical practices.

The factors that brought about these highly desirable decreases in the acute infective diseases have been in addition to the purification of the water supplies – improved sanitation, better housing, the provision of more air and sunlight and the reduction of overcrowding, with generally improved nutrition and higher standards of living. The deformation of bone growth due to rickets was woefully evident before the discovery of vitamins at the time of the First World War. The significance of these facts concerning fevers and bone disease will be considered in a later chapter. The twentieth century has witnessed great advances in the science of nutrition, but, regretfully, this does not mean that most people's dietary is free from error. The reasons for this discrepancy, which is a cause of much present-day trouble, will also be considered in a later chapter.

Are We Living Longer?

Nowadays, much is made of the claim that the increase in life-expectation is an indication of improved health, but here again the position is not one of unreserved satisfaction. The facts show that, whereas during the nineteenth century life-expectation *at birth* was as low as 35 years, now it is about double that figure. This improvement has resulted from the very great reduction of deaths from the acute infections, as already noted, and a very large reduction in infant mortality brought about by improved sanitation and the vastly improved care for mother and baby in childbirth. In other words, fewer people die young. Also, generally improved nutrition has brought about increased resistance to infection. Whereas in the nineteenth century infant mortality in the first year of life was very great (even at the end of the nineteenth century a large percentage of the population died before the age of twenty), those who survived to adulthood include those who are now in their eighties, nineties, and even a proportion of centenarians. Among the killer diseases of those times, tuberculosis has almost been eliminated with the improved standard of life and, in particular, of nutrition.

Many people are surprised to learn that, at the age of 45, life-expectation is very little higher than it was at the beginning of the century, while life-expectation at the age of 65 has not increased at all; in fact it is tending to decrease rather than increase, both in Great Britain and the USA, even with the development of improved geriatric medicine, including better shelter and care of the aged, as well as the very costly units for resuscitation and intensive care in cardiac failure, renal failure and other emergencies.

In fact, apart from acute illnesses such as influenza and the common cold, the great majority of health problems today arise from the diseases of degeneration, chiefly coronary and other forms of thrombosis and strokes (which mainly result from degeneration of blood-vessels), cancer, chronic bronchitis, and (the most widespread group of all) arthritis and other forms of rheumatism. Increasing numbers of sufferers, from middle age onward, are having to be cared for by hospitals, nursing homes or members of the patient's family in varying conditions of physical and in some cases also mental deterioration which have been referred to as 'a state of medicated survival'. Most of these unfortunates are also suffering from some form of arthritis, many in an advanced stage of the disease.

In seeking the solution to a problem, particularly in the field of the vital processes of health and disease, it is most likely that a satisfactory solution will appear only when the study includes all relevant factors. Thus, in addition to physiological observations, the ecological factors must be thoroughly evaluated, namely the possible stress factors arising from the exterior environment, plus everything that goes into the body, our food, chemicals (including drugs), and other pollutants from 'airs, waters and places'.

The acute diseases of earlier times have been related to harmful unhygienic factors in the external environment as well as in the internal environment, where some degree of malnutrition has been involved.

One of the Greatest Medical Errors

In the nineteenth century one of the greatest errors of medicine was the literal acceptance of the germ theory, which led to the concentration on the theory of chemotherapy — 'kill the germ and cure the disease'. To some extent this idea still persists. In the history of medicine there have been many instances where an error of oversimplification has obscured the perception of other vital factors.

In all the accord given to the work of Pasteur, it is seldom mentioned that some of the most eminent and sincere men of his day were unable to accept the germ theory in its oversimplified form. Neither is it generally mentioned that ultimately Pasteur himself came to perceive that germs were far from being the sole cause of disease, infectious or otherwise; indeed, he actually taught that the healthy body is proof against the attacks of germs and, further, towards the end of his life he stated to Professor Renon (his medical attendant): 'Claude Bernard was right. The germ is nothing – the soil is everything.' In his use of the word 'soil' he meant the condition of the body and its environment.

Today it is still imperative that, in this wider sense, *causes* must be strictly related to *effects* if progress towards better health and the effective treatment of disease is to be achieved.

The role of bacteria in the virulent infective diseases has now been largely superseded by the ubiquitous 'virus infections'. Similar views of possible specific viral causation govern the ever-continuing researches concerning colds and influenza, etc. – research which, after many years, has proved to be singularly unsuccessful.

Likewise, after many years and large sums of money spent in research, sufferers from arthritis and other rheumatic diseases are persistently told by their doctors that the cause of rheumatism is not known and so no cure has been produced. Once again, medicine appears to be seeking something which is likely to be an oversimplification – a specific cause to be resolved by a specific remedy, presumably a drug. If the biologists would take their eyes from the microscope long enough they might recognise the existence of a multiplicity of causes resulting in varied and fluctuating symptoms, all leading towards the well-known degenerative changes associated with these diseases.

The great majority of our germs live with us happily and healthily in a balanced state known as 'symbiosis' (see pp. 14 and 110).

CHAPTER 7

Causes and Effects
1: The Dynamic Basis of Health

Vast expenditure on research establishments over many years has failed to produce a rational cause or a specific cure for rheumatic diseases. Why?

Gradually it is being realised that there are numerous possible causes and there can be no single cure.

In order to understand the nature of these causes some knowledge of the body's vital processes is essential.

It is freely admitted by the medical profession that no cure and no specific cause have been found for arthritis and rheumatic troubles in general, in spite of the very considerable sums which have been devoted to research programmes, decade after decade. This means that no specific medical treatment can be offered for these diseases.

Furthermore, there are distinct indications that, however learnedly, elaborately and expensively the present forms of research may be pursued, rheumatic diseases, the common cold and most of the other chronic degenerative diseases will still be with us as long as the researchers' aim is to circumvent the natural causes of these disease conditions. Thus, it is vainly hoped that a remedy, a 'magic bullet' may emerge which will exempt patients from undertaking measures of self help related to the various contributory causes which have evidently been involved in the development of their particular form of rheumatic ailment.

In a later chapter, such a course of treatment related to natural causes will be described. Among those who choose to follow these treatments there may be some who will adhere to the recommended procedures without question, but probably a majority will expect to be given a rational explanation before adopting a form of treatment which involves certain measures of self-help. Such an explanation may make it easier to accept the absolute need for certain changes of habits and activities if we clarify the reasons why such changes are essential if progress and ultimate success are to be achieved.

It is also to be hoped that people who are not yet suffering from such troubles, but who witness the suffering and disablement of others less fortunate, may be induced to find in these ways the means of avoiding similar troubles, realising that prevention is better than cure. To the latter it may be said that such misfortunes are not inevitable, particularly if they will accept the fact that the only sure means of prevention lie within themselves, recognising the causes of arthritic conditions and acting accordingly to avoid them. To this end, there is a need to have some practical knowledge of the laws of nature as they concern our health and well-being. This does not mean that a detailed knowledge of anatomy and physiology is required, but there *are* certain basic facts and principles which all of us might do well to understand.

It is a universally accepted principle that when something happens which may be termed an *effect* it must be due to something else which is the *cause*. This principle applies particularly in matters of health and disease, where we may expect cause and effect to be strictly related, either directly or indirectly. An effect may be due to a single cause or to several causes. One of the main pitfalls encountered in the medical search for disease causation is oversimplification – the search for a *single* cause as, for example, in the case of the germ theory of disease which has already been mentioned.

In contrast with ills with a single cause, for example direct poisoning, the great majority of modern ills almost invariably arise from multiple causation, and this is true of the rheumatic diseases. Even in cases of traumatic arthritis which has followed some specific injury there are other factors which determine the severity and ultimate course and degree of recovery from the initial traumatic occurrence. While there has been a dramatic decline in the incidence and the virulence of the acute fevers which were formerly so prevalent (Figure 1, page 33), there has occurred a similar decline in the incidence and virulence of the acute form of rheumatism, rheumatic fever, which may be ascribed to similar causes. In the official publication *Rheumatism and Arthritis in Britain* it is stated: 'The prevalence of rheumatic fever has been much reduced during this century because of improved living conditions, although that of rheumatic heart disease has not yet fallen. Prevention by antibiotics is possible, but once rheumatic fever has developed they are of little value.'

These statements may seem to be somewhat confusing, but the overall picture of health and disease becomes much clearer if we consider certain implications of natural processes and in particular the phenomenon which has already been mentioned (p. 24), namely *homoeostasis,* a word derived from the Greek and literally meaning 'constant state'. The condition of the living body is not a static but a

38

dynamic one with very many processes in a state of ever-changing activity, including reactions to changes in our external environment and with varying simultaneous activities and exchanges taking place in our internal environment which is composed of the tissue fluid, lymph, and blood.

The composition of these body fluids and numerous other factors in the living body must remain in a steady state within very narrow limits, for any departure from these limits immediately constitutes a challenge to health, and even to life itself, as also do the stresses to which changes in our external environment may subject us.

The following are some examples of the most important of these vital conditions for life and health.

1 Body Temperature

The temperature of the body is normally about 98·4° F (37° C) and it will remain close to this level whether we are in a tropical environment of 100° F or more or in an arctic region many degrees below freezing-point. The operation of this wonderful control involves modification of the continuous processes whereby the blood circulation is speeded or slowed, together with variations in the speed and strength of the heart-beat, the redistribution of blood throughout the system, the constriction or expansion of blood-vessels, and the opening or closing of the pores and the sweat glands in the skin. The increased volume of blood brought to the skin in hot weather is cooled by the evaporation of the sweat, and the reverse of these processes conserves heat in response to external cold. The exquisite processes of temperature control are effected by a special part of the brain which acts as a thermostat, and its working is independent of any conscious control on our part.

2 Acid-alkali Balance

Equally elegant and efficient are the biochemical mechanisms which control the acid/alkali balance of the blood. For those who are not conversant with chemistry this balance is measured by what is referred to as the pH scale. The neutral point, where acid and alkali exactly balance on this scale is pH 7. Fluids with a pH greater than 7 are alkaline, while those below pH 7 are acid. It is essential to life that the blood shall be slightly alkaline, maintained approximately at a figure of pH 7·4. If the blood pH falls below this figure, i.e. to a level close to pH 7, we are said to suffer from a relative acidosis. Even small variations under 7·4 are dangerous and if the pH falls only to 7·0 there is an immediate risk of coma and death. Conversely, if blood alkalinity rises only to pH 7·8 this is sufficient to produce convulsions.

Later in this book various factors will be described which may tend to disturb the critical acid/alkali balance in one direction or the other. The maintenance of pH within such narrow limits is achieved by the interaction between the gas, carbon dioxide (CO_2), and the alkaline compound sodium bicarbonate (the same substance as is used for baking-powder). When the blood reaches the lungs carbon dioxide is expelled in the process of breathing. Thus the strength and rapidity of the heart-beat and the speed and depth of breathing are automatically matched to the need of the moment to expel carbon dioxide.

3 Sugar in the Blood

In addition to these finely regulated processes of the body there are numerous others, equally remarkable, all of which are designed to preserve the balance of health within fine limits – a provision of nature which is well termed 'homoeostasis'. Among the most important of these is the control of the sugar content of the blood. This, like the others, is subject to dual control by the nervous system in conjunction with hormones secreted by various glands, and specifically with the hormone *insulin,* which serves to control the storage of sugar in the liver and in the muscles. The failure of this process results in the increasingly common disease of diabetes.

4 Fluid Balance and the Kidneys

The maintenance of fluid balance is also of vital importance, the water content of the body being directly related to the factors of pH and the concentrations of other solvents in the plasma and tissue fluid. It is one of the critical factors in relation to rheumatic troubles. Although the margin of safety is wider than in the three processes already described, it is of no less importance ultimately in relation to these and other factors affecting the balance of health.

The human body normally consists of 60–70 per cent water by weight, of which about 75 per cent is inside the living cells and is termed the *intracellular* fluid. The remainder, termed the *extracellular* fluid, is contained in the spaces between the cells as tissue fluid or *lymph* and in the blood as *plasma* and also as very specialised fluids such as the digestive juices and the fluids which lubricate and convey nourishment to the joints. These are the fluids which Claude Bernard called the *milieu interne,* and which Cannon called the *fluid matrix,* the all-important *internal environment,* the constant state of which (homoeostasis) is essential for the life of all our many millions of living cells. The lymph passes through an elaborate system of vessels and lymphatic glands and re-enters the bloodstream.

These fluids, carrying their precious load of all the materials of life, are in a state of constant movement, bringing oxygen and nutrients absorbed from the digestive system and removing carbon dioxide and tissue wastes which are subsequently excreted. That the margin of safety of the water content of the body is wider than in certain other bodily control mechanisms is due mainly to the work of the kidneys.

We possess only one heart and one liver, but two kidneys – a fact which emphasises the vital importance of the elaborate biochemical programme which the hard-working kidneys perform, normally with great exactitude and efficiency.

How does the kidney work? It is appropriate to gain some simple understanding as to how this seemingly miraculous work is performed so that the reader may appreciate the need, and have something of the know-how, to avoid damage and premature degeneration of these vitally important organs. *Some degree of loss of kidney efficiency is frequently associated with chronic rheumatism.*

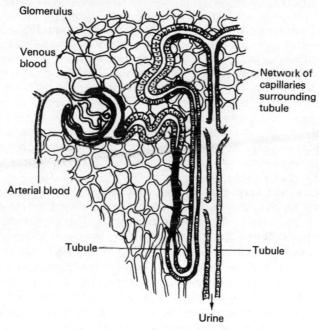

2   The nephron

The unit of the kidney is the *nephron* which, greatly magnified, is illustrated in Figure 2. There are between 1 and 1¼ million nephrons in each kidney and as the blood flows through them at about 2½ pints per minute a number of vital processes are performed by the healthy kidney with great efficiency. The principal functions are as follows:

(a) The bulbous capsule, the *glomerulus,* filters and purifies the blood as it passes through a dense network of tiny blood capillaries in the capsule. Blood cells and large protein molecules in the plasma are retained because of their size and the filtered fluid then passes on to the next process, which takes place in the tubules.

(b) It is known that as much as 45 gallons of fluid passes into the tubules after filtration. If all this fluid were excreted as urine the result would, of course, be fatally disastrous, but the filtrate undergoes complicated and precise processing in its passage through the tubules, so that only about 2 or 3 pints emerge as urine, the excess being passed back into the bloodstream via the complex of blood capillaries which surround the tubules. In this way the kidney is primarily responsible for the *water balance* of the whole body.

(c) In addition to controlling the water balance, the tubules are primarily involved in preserving the acid/alkali balance (pH) of the blood.

(d) The processes of fluid retention and reabsorption effected in the tubules also serve to avoid losses of essential substances such as amino-acids (which are the basis of protein synthesis), proteins and glucose. This process of conservation in the tubules also regulates the concentrations in the blood of the numerous mineral salts (electrolytes), the loss of which would give rise to serious deficiencies. The process also extends to the conservation of the so-called 'trace elements' which, although present in extremely small amounts, are needed for some special function, for example a minute trace of cobalt incorporated in the molecule of Vitamin B12, and of copper for the synthesis of blood cells, etc.

(e) Less well known is the fact that nature, with characteristic economy, utilises the kidneys as a site for chemical synthesis by means of which an enzyme named *renin* is secreted. This enzyme helps to control blood pressure. Another enzyme, *erythropoietin,* is produced in the kidneys. This enzyme stimulates the production of new blood cells.

(f) As a result of the action of the tubules, many unwanted and in some instances poisonous substances are prevented from re-entering the bloodstream and, instead, are voided in the urine. This may include toxic chemicals from the external environment, including many of the drugs which are prescribed so freely today, all of which are liable to find their way to the long-suffering kidneys.

42

Kidneys under Attack

The stresses imposed upon the kidneys under present-day civilised conditions are evinced in the large and increasing number of cases of renal insufficiency and failure. It is not generally recognised that progressive impairment of the kidneys is a major cause of the modern prevalence of degenerative diseases.

It is significant that most of the drugs in use are known to be potentially a cause of kidney damage.

5 Oxygen Control

It will be noted that while some homoeostatic mechanisms are concerned with vital processes, others are concerned with specific substances. In the latter category comes the control of oxygen. While we may live several days without water and weeks without food, survival without oxygen is a matter of minutes and in as short a time as eight minutes irreversible damage is done to brain cells. Also the body's oxygen requirement varies enormously. At rest, it may be as small as 0·3 litres per minute, whereas in severe exertion the need will rise to 15 litres and in very severe exertion may rise to as much as 60 litres per minute. These characteristics of varying oxygen need obviously require great efficiency in the mechanisms controlling oxygen requirements at any particular time. These varying requirements are met by complex processes in which oxygen supply is linked to blood neutrality (pH). The working muscle develops lactic acid in proportion to the degree of exertion. This is oxidised to carbon dioxide (CO_2), which in solution forms carbonic acid (H_2CO_3), which circulates in the blood. The increase of CO_2 then stimulates a breathing centre in the brain which causes breathing to become more rapid and deep so that extra oxygen is taken in while excess CO_2 is exhaled in the process of expiration. All these reactions are effected by means of specific enzymes, which are produced in the body for this purpose.

The degree of efficiency of these respiratory processes has a considerable bearing on our health.

6 Essential Minerals

Among the many other substances which must be controlled according to the requirements of homoeostasis are the numerous essential minerals. Sodium and potassium are of first importance, because, in addition to ensuring the alkalinity of the blood and effecting the transmission of nerve impulses, they are also involved in a

43

number of other important biological processes. Potassium is present in all cells, being known as the cell salt, while sodium is the tissue fluid salt. The conservation of both sodium and potassium is accomplished during the passage of the tissue fluid through the kidney tubules and, in common with the other constituents of the filtered fluid, normal amounts are returned to the blood while unwanted excesses are voided in the urine.

7 The Importance of Calcium

The concentration of calcium in the bloodstream for the requirements of homoeostasis is equally important. It is concerned in a number of biological and anatomical functions which, if impaired, are closely related to the possible onset of rheumatic ailments, including arthritis.

Compounds of the metal calcium are involved in some of the body's most important reactions, both chemical and structural. In the form of its salt, calcium phosphate, it supplies the hardening material of the bones and teeth and is involved in the growth and repair of bone. In view of the fact that dead bones may be discovered in the earth in a state of preservation centuries after the remainder of the body has been completely decomposed, it might be supposed that the bones in the living body, once formed, are stable, but in fact there is a lifelong exchange of calcium between bone and blood. While about 99 per cent of the body's calcium is in the bones and teeth, the relatively small amount of calcium in the blood is of vital importance, being maintained normally at about 10 milligrams per 100 grams with great precision. A lowering of blood calcium will produce cramps and twitchings of muscle and eventually convulsions, while an abnormal increase in blood calcium will increase blood viscosity and may cause deposition of calcium in parts of the body where they are not wanted.

In addition to the role of calcium in the growth and maintenance of bones and teeth, the clotting of blood, and thus the control of haemorrhage, is dependent upon the calcium in the blood. Also calcium is a vital component of cell membranes and an essential factor in muscle contraction and nerve impulses, and in the secretion of hormones by certain of the endocrine glands.

The homoeostatic control of calcium is of such importance that four small endocrine glands – the parathyroids (situated in the front of the neck close to the thyroid gland) – control calcium metabolism in conjunction with vitamin D. The thyroid and pituitary glands also exert a controlling influence over the complex metabolism of calcium.

This chapter briefly describes what is known of the main vital processes and essential substances which must be spontaneously controlled if the balance of health is to be maintained. It also gives some indications of the ways in which these controls are effected. Not a single one of the many homoeostatic mechanisms is an isolated process. In the next chapter, the manner in which these mechanisms are welded into a harmonious whole is considered. As with all complex mechanisms, it must be recognised that *the whole is greater than the sum of the parts.*

The Medical Mystique

As already mentioned, many doctors hold the opinion that patients and other laymen should not expect to receive much information concerning health matters or to be told more than the barest facts about the nature of their illness, and even less about the treatments prescribed. Thus, there has been created what has been termed the 'medical mystique', as if such self-knowledge and understanding is beyond the grasp of the lay mind.

In contrast with this attitude, the exponents of natural therapy believe that factual information and explanation are helpful to success in carrying out the methods of self-help based on self-knowledge which are essential to achieve lasting benefit in all forms of rheumatism and arthritis. Such self-help is equally essential in the prevention of these distressing diseases, as well as their cure.

Here, then, are some further facts which the reader may find both interesting and instructive.

CHAPTER 8

Causes and Effects
2: Safeguards, Responses
and Defences

Normally a highly complex and purposeful series of reactions is in constant activity within us, ready to respond to the functional needs of every part or organ at any moment of our life.

These active functions are spontaneous and mainly without our conscious control. Symptoms begin to appear when this happy balance of health is disturbed.

The many and varied ways in which the human body maintains so many biochemical and physical factors within strict limits, as outlined in the previous chapter, must not be regarded as a collection of isolated processes. On the contrary, they are all monitored and directed into a harmonious whole under a primary system of versatile dual overall biochemical control, in which the system of endocrine glands and the nervous system co-operate.

This sensitive dual control normally acts and reacts so as to secure lifelong adaptation and compensation to all the many disturbing and frequently hostile influences (both external and internal) in our environment which we experience in our day-to-day life. Furthermore, these homoeostatic regulatory defences act protectively in most of the fluctuating stresses of life with which we may have to contend, possibly even up to the extreme limits of the competitive athlete.

These powers of *response* to the many demands imposed upon the body are made possible only through the interdependence of the dual adaptive mechanisms of hormones and nerves. Concerning the endocrine glands, the primary response to stress is the secretion of adrenalin by the adrenal glands which are situated at the top of each kidney, but it should be understood that the activity of one type of gland also to some degree involves the others.

Thus the endocrine gland system includes the pituitary, the adrenals, the thyroid, the parathyroids and the ovaries and testes, each of which secretes its specific hormone or hormones. The total action of these 'chemical messengers' is often referred to as the 'endocrine orchestra' while the pituitary gland, which is situated close to the mid-brain, has been termed 'the leader of the orchestra'.

The Dual Control of Nerves

The other equally essential partner in this dual control system is that part of the nervous system which is termed the *autonomic nervous system*. The term autonomic, means 'self-controlling', and refers to the fact that this very important system of nerves governs those very many functions of which, under normal circumstances, we are not conscious and over which we have no voluntary control. Among many examples of these subconscious functions are the control of the heart-rate, the active movements of the stomach and intestines in the work of digestion and excretion, the contraction and expansion of blood-vessels, the mechanics of the urinary system, the sweat glands and numerous other glands and their secretions.

The word 'nerves' is commonly used in the sense of emotions such as depression, overexcitement, fears, frustrations, etc., thus leading to the false assumption that nervous disorders are mainly, if not entirely, imaginary and that they have nothing to do with the complex physical system which motivates our every vital activity. Such misconceptions may mean that the sufferer from nervous disorder, who may be in a state of distress and perhaps in very real pain, will be given such valueless advice as to 'pull himself together' or 'forget it' or 'snap out of it'. This sort of misconception may frequently occur with those suffering from rheumatism, particularly in cases where disability is less obvious but no less distressing to the sufferer.

It may therefore lead to a clearer understanding of the involvement of the nerves in all rheumatic conditions if a brief description of the nervous system is given. Also it will indicate a logical and effective approach to treatment. The diagrammatic sketches (Figures 3 and 4) illustrate both the central nervous system (Figure 3) and the autonomic nervous system (see Figure 4 on page 49). The central nervous system consists of the brain and its extension, the spinal cord, which are protectively situated in the skull and the spine respectively. The nerve cells in the brain and cord are termed *neurones* and they are comparatively large cells. From each of these neurones nerve fibres extend to serve all parts of the body. There are many millions of neurones and corresponding numbers of nerve fibres which are enclosed in 12 pairs of cranial nerves and 31 pairs of spinal nerves. Some of these fibres in every nerve send messages to the brain conveying essential information such as sensations of heat, cold, pain, touch and pressure and, in the case of the cranial nerves, sight, hearing,

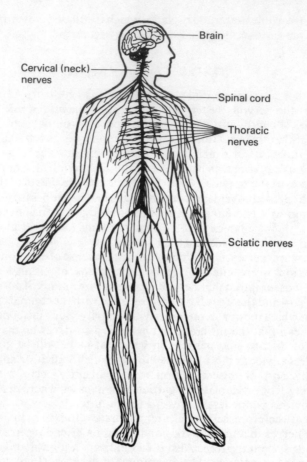

Brain

Cervical (neck) nerves

Spinal cord

Thoracic nerves

Sciatic nerves

3   The central nervous system

taste, smell, etc. Others, termed the 'motor nerves', are responsible for voluntary muscle control. These latter are known as the voluntary nerves because they are subject to our conscious control.

Even in these voluntary muscle movements, however, nature operates an overriding spontaneous device – the spinal reflex which causes us to withdraw instantly and involuntarily in emergency situations, for example withdrawing the hand or foot in response to sudden pain, or the sharp recovery of balance following a slip or stumble. In addition to these, there are known to be numerous other protective reflexes of which we are usually quite unaware.

48

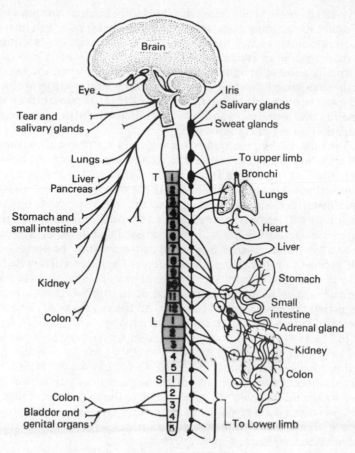

4   The automatic nervous system

Figure 4 indicates something of the nature and functional scope of the autonomic nervous system, which acts as an efficient 'manager' of the great number of spontaneous activities of virtually all our parts and organs, so that happily we may be able to pursue our occupations and interests undistracted by the many essential vital processes which should normally proceed silently and efficiently.

The autonomic nervous system itself is in two divisions, namely the *sympathetic* and the *parasympathetic*. These two divisions exert opposing and reciprocal functions, so that an activity which is 'switched on' by one division will be 'switched off', modified or reversed by the other division, thus enabling this dual nervous system to adapt to our immediate needs at any particular time. For instance, if, in response to a call for action, the sympathetic nerves stimulate certain specific active functions, then parasympathetic nerves will normally subdue or inhibit the same functions when the need for action has passed. Normally, also, these opposing controls are ideally adjusted to our needs so that the transition from one state of activity to another will progress smoothly and efficiently with the minimum intrusion upon our consciousness.

Thus, in general, the sympathetic system may be said to cater for external activity and to respond to stress – processes often popularly expressed as 'preparing for flight or fight'. If, for instance, extra physical effort is needed, the sympathetic impulses cause the heart to beat faster and stronger, blood pressure will rise proportionately, breathing will become more rapid and deep and hormone secretions, in particular adrenalin, will be increased, while what are called vegetative functions such as digestive processes will be decreased by the action of the parasympathetic nerves. The latter will reverse these effects when the demands of stress are past, reactivating vegetative functions such as digestion and assimilation of food and otherwise adjusting the physiological functions to the requirements of a more peaceful but no less important level of activity.

In Figure 4 (page 49), one half of the sympathetic system is shown on the right of the diagram, while on the left one half of the parasympathetic system is indicated. In the case of the sympathetic nerves the cell junctions (shown in the diagram as a series of black dots) are not within the spine but lie very close to the spine on each side. The cell junctions receive connections to and from the corresponding spinal segments which then pass via further large nerve centres (the *ganglia*) to terminate in specific organs.

The parasympathetic system, half of which is shown on the diagram, is not provided with a chain of cell unctions as is the sympathetic system, the major part of the former division being the extensive complex known as the *vagus* nerve (the term *vagus* means wandering) which arises directly from the brain, its branches being widely distributed throughout the body.

Despite, and mainly because of, their opposing functions, the sympathetic and parasympathetic divisions act together, and also normally in conjunction with the central nervous system, to provide a normally perfect service in accordance with our needs and desires in all the usual – and even in many of the unusual – activities of our life. One of the most important of the many activities of the autonomic nervous system concerns the control of glandular secretions, including the endocrine glands, which secrete a variety of hormones, each of which serves as a specific 'chemical messenger'.

The Immune Response

A further and very active and important response is the ultimate defensive reaction known as the *immune response*. It is now common knowledge that materials with which our body structures are built are *proteins*. In fact the basic materials of *all* living creatures, from microbes to man, are proteins. Even our bones are a matrix of protein hardened by the deposition of calcium. The properties of these extremely complex compounds are truly remarkable.

Proteins are essentially composed of the atoms of carbon, hydrogen, oxygen and nitrogen which are arranged in many combinations to form very large and complex molecular structures, thus presenting the possibility of an infinite number of variations and permutations. A protein molecule may also incorporate other elements such as phosphorus, sulphur and small amounts of certain metals, etc.

The simplest small molecules from which proteins are built are called *amino-acids*. Thus when we eat proteins in our food our digestive system breaks down the ingested proteins to amino-acids which are then rebuilt by the biochemical processes of metabolism to form human protein. The amazing thing is that, while proteins are the structural materials of us all, *each individual's protein is peculiar to himself* and it differs from everyone else's protein (with rare exceptions, such as identical twins). Resulting from this diversity of protein structure is the fact that the body has the ability to recognise and tolerate its own proteins so as not to react against them. If, however, a foreign protein should enter the body a defensive reaction will be mounted against it in order to reject it. This is the *immune response*. The invading protein is termed an *antigen* and the body responds by producing defensive substances termed *antibodies,* which themselves are complex protein molecules. Also, certain cells such as *leucocytes* (white blood cells) and *plasma cells* are involved in the defence reactions aimed at destroying antigens, such as harmful invading microbes, by process named *phagocytosis* (literally meaning 'eating up cells').

It should be observed that, in some cases, non-protein substances, including antibiotics such as penicillin, may provoke an immune response. Closely related to the immune response are the familiar reactions of *fever* (in which there is a general rise in body temperature) and *inflammation* (which generally is a localised reaction). The

51

significance of these responsive reactions as they affect treatment will be considered in a later chapter. They are very potent vital processes which may serve to restore normality and repair tissue damage, especially if they are treated in ways which assist their natural functions.

In this chapter and the preceding chapter we describe in the simplest possible terms the spontaneous processes and mechanisms upon which depends our day-to-day survival and which are the means by which our health and well-being are sustained. These powers are subject to the natural laws of cause and effect. In response to our environmental conditions, both internal and external, and to our habits of life, the success or failure of these defences will inevitably determine our eventual state of health or disease. Being the possessors of these miraculous powers, we cannot escape the consequences if we constantly transgress the laws of health upon which our vital processes depend.

Health – Our Inescapable Responsibility

Thus, we learn that to a great degree we have an inescapable responsibility in matters affecting our personal problems of health and disease. Only when we know something of the vital processes may we fully appreciate the practical purposes of these inborn powers of healing, repair and maintenance.

Having been shown how the diseases of times past have been related to environmental factors and habits of life, it may be easy for the reader to understand why countless attempts to find a 'wonder remedy', which would absolve the sufferer from personal responsibility without regard to the causes of his condition, have constantly failed to achieve their objective. Similar fallacies and delusive ideas still continue to obscure the issue of present-day disease causation. From Hippocrates onward, in one era and another, there have been wise and unprejudiced doctors who have called, often vainly, for a more logical relation of causes to effects in the study of the nature of health and the treatment of disease.

A recent appeal for truth and common sense has come from no less an authority than Sir Harold Evans, Chairman of the Health Education Council, 78 New Oxford Street, London WC1, who is reported (*Daily Telegraph,* 27 August 1976) as stating that: 'The killer diseases of the past and the conditions in which they flourished were now under control, but new ones had taken their place.' In the Council's annual report he said that 'Much of today's diseases are man-made and avoidable. People put themselves at risk through ignorance, bad advice, laziness and self-indulgence.

'Let us knock our bodies about if we must, but do not let it happen out of ignorance. Into the balance, let us also put the possible consequences for our families together with the cost to the community in patching up our bodies.'

The profound changes in our way of life resulting from the development of our so-called Western civilisation are undoubtedly related to the changes in the forms of disease, this being a fact to be borne in mind in defining the possible causes of what are now recognised as being 'the most widespread group of diseases known to man.'

Chemotherapy fails to meet the challenge of today's diseases. There exists a valid alternative and the further facts given in the next chapter may help to decide your choice.

Chemotherapy fails to restore health because it attempts to treat the human system with a remedy for each symptom. Too often the result is a state of confusion and the onset of progressive degeneration.

The natural alternative is whole-person treatment directed to resolving the real causes of disease.

CHAPTER 9

Human Ecology –
The Neglected Science

*Positive health and fitness and freedom from disease are not to
be bought. No millionaire can secure his health, even though his
physician may be in constant attention, unless he is prepared to
help himself.*

*A wise doctor will advise accordingly, admitting that no
panacea, no 'magic remedy', exists. This applies to rich and poor
alike. The guidelines for effective self-help may be regarded as an
exercise in the science of human ecology.*

Costly researches in the fields of biology, physiology, anatomy and
pathology have yielded much information concerning the intricate
workings and structure of the human body but they have contributed
relatively little in the way of satisfactory solutions to the present-day
problems of health and disease. This, however, is an aspect of life in
which modern man is greatly in need of help and guidance. Compared
with previous centuries, his present life situation appears to be more
sheltered, he is more affluent and he has been given free access to a
costly health service the like of which has never previously existed.

Despite all these benefits, the principal causes of premature death
are associated with tissue degeneration of the circulatory system
(coronary thrombosis, strokes and varicose veins) and of the
respiratory system (bronchitis, emphysema, asthma and pneumonia),
and with failure of vital organs such as kidneys, liver, pancreas, etc.,
while the quality of life is becoming progressively impaired for the vast
number of sufferers from rheumatic disorders. Over all lies the shadow
of the most lethal of the degenerative diseases – cancer.

The reasons for this present failure of medical research lie, broadly
speaking, in the fact that most of our problems of health and disease
are very much less likely to be solved by means of the microscopes and
test tubes of the laboratory than through a relatively neglected science,
namely in the field of human ecology.

What is Ecology?

The *New English Encyclopedia* defines 'ecology' as 'the branch of biology that studies the relationship between organisms and their environment, especially the mutual dependence of living organisms in any area. It has been defined as "biological economics" and is concerned with the ways in which any community of organisms maintains a balance so that its members continue to flourish.' It follows that if human communities are to achieve their highest potential and flourish they must establish a balanced relationship with their environment. The inborn adaptive mechanisms described briefly in Chapters 7 and 8 have been developed and maintained over many thousands of years of man's existence. Where these mechanisms have suffered disturbance or breakdown, ecological factors have been mainly responsible.

Modern civilisation, with its dominant industrial system, has introduced environmental factors the nature of which has never before been experienced. This has profoundly altered modern man's habits of life, creating many new forms of stress to which, to a great extent, he has not fully adapted. To some extent, and in many different ways, this affects us all, and unless we are able to achieve a much-improved degree of adaptation the outlook is far from promising, particularly as our civilisation is no longer merely 'Western', having spread its influence to the point where only small and still shrinking minorities remain unaffected by its influence.

The problems are ecological ones, in face of which the science of ecology assumes primary importance.

We may consider Hippocrates as having been in his day a master of ecology. In the present century, those who have accepted the Hippocratic principle of seeking the causes of disease in the habits of the individual and his environmental relationships are to be found among some of the more learned, thoughtful physicians, including medical scientists of world-wide fame. Dr Alexis Carrel, of the Rockefeller Insitute of Medical Research, a Nobel prize winner, in his book *Man the Unknown,* appeared as one of those who appreciated the fallacies of modern scientific medicine. Carrel recognised the causes of modern degenerative diseases and the need to relate curative and preventive measures to these causes.

Professor René Dubos, also of the famous Rockefeller Institute, has developed these and similar themes in several books, including *Man Adapting* and *Man, Medicine and Environment.*

The eminent surgeon, Sir Arbuthnot Lane, stated fifty years ago: 'Long surgical experience has proved to me conclusively that there is something radically and fundamentally wrong with the civilized mode of life, and I believe that unless the present dietetic and health customs and habits of the White Nations are reorganized, social decay and race

55

deterioration are inevitable.' These and other medical scientists, endeavouring to gain understanding of the nature and causes of health and disease, have been largely concerned to study the effects of what we absorb from our external environment and what enters our internal environment – first and foremost our food. Among the most important workers in this field have been Sir Robert McCarrison and Dr Weston Price.

Not Much Work for the Doctor

McCarrison qualified as a medical practitioner at Queen's University, Belfast, in 1900. At the age of twenty-three he entered the Indian Medical Service and while agency surgeon at Gilgit in the north of India he was greatly impressed with the exceptionally good health and physique of the people of Hunza, who lived in an isolated valley in the great mountains of that region. While being their sole doctor for some seven years he was able to verify what others before him had reported, namely a total absence of the diseases of civilisation. Apart from attending to accidental injuries he found no troubles to treat other than some seasonal eye trouble which was ascribed to the effect of the smoke-laden atmosphere of their ill ventilated houses in the very harsh winters of that region. He found their span of life to be extraordinarily long with marked absence of degenerative changes. McCarrison concluded that their dietary was the major factor in maintaining freedom from disease and a state of physical excellence.

In his book *Nutrition and Health* McCarrison stated: 'Their sole food consists of grains, vegetables and fruits with a certain amount of milk and butter. Meat was rarely eaten, their available land being so limited they were not able to keep more livestock than goats which browse on the hills.'

In 1918 McCarrison returned to India under the Research Fund Association of India. He examined the dietaries of many of the races of India and found that their food was closely related to the incidence and types of diseases from which each region suffered. In the usual manner of medical research the respective dietaries were fed to laboratory rats. Those animals fed on the healthful diets of Hunzas and Sikhs flourished and remained free from disease, while those animals fed on the poorest Indian diets of the people of Madras and Travancore were stunted in growth and developed diseases similar to the corresponding human diseases in each area. Moreover, rats fed on a typical poor European dietary suffered similar patterns of disease.

Dr Weston Price, a member of the Research Commission of the American Dental Association, was commissioned to investigate

56

isolated communities in order to find out why primitive races have good teeth and, if possible, why their teeth decayed after they became 'civilised'. In a world-wide tour of field studies Dr Price established beyond doubt that not only their teeth but also their standards of physical excellence and freedom from civilised diseases were directly related to their native, unprocessed natural foods. In the course of his journeys he examined thousands of individuals and supported his findings with thousands of photographs, a large number of which were reproduced in his book. In addition, thousands of these native diets were sent for analysis and were constantly found to have a high content of the essential food factors, vitamins, minerals, etc., providing at least four times the USA official standards of normal body requirements. In some cases the increase was as much as tenfold compared with typical European and USA dietaries.

Dr Price Finds the Answer

It should be appreciated that these are the food factors which confer high *natural immunity* to infection and freedom from degenerative diseases. The evidence obtained by means of this very large field study was presented by Dr Weston Price in his book *Nutrition and Physical Degeneration.* It has been repeatedly shown that following the introduction into primitive communities of commercially processed foods, as a result of which natural traditional foods were largely replaced by white flour products, refined sugar, polished rice and other processed and artificially preserved foods, signs of dental caries and evidence of our civilised degenerative diseases begin to appear. Then, and only then, did Weston Price report cases of rheumatic disease.

In his report Price stated: 'Careful inquiry regarding the presence of arthritis was made in the more isolated groups. We neither saw nor heard of a case in the isolated groups. However, at the point of contact with the foods of modern civilization many cases were found.'

Some twelve years ago correspondence appeared in the *British Medical Journal* pleading that further field researches should be carried out to establish and record the facts concerning the health status in the few remaining and rapidly diminishing primitive communities before the march of our civilisation introduces what are termed our 'sophisticated' foods into the lives of these peoples. It was pleaded that without such further surveys future generations of doctors will find it difficult to believe the remarkable facts and figures obtained in surveys already carried out and reported. As far as I know, no such follow-up survey project has been carried out. Furthermore, it is very probable that any such exposition would meet with a reception among the majority of doctors as lukewarm or as cold as hitherto. In general, their interest is more likely to focus on the latest information supplied by the manufacturers of the newest 'wonder drug'.

CHAPTER 10

The Natural Way to Health

The natural treatment of rheumatic and arthritic diseases is not an adjunct to orthodox chemotherapy. It is the valid alternative which will best promote healing and repair.

The dangers and disadvantages of drug treatment should be fully realised. If the directions for self-help are meticulously followed, distressing symptoms should be progressively eased so that symptom-suppressing 'wonder drugs' should be rendered superfluous.

In Chapters 4 and 5 the persistence of two schools of medical thought and practice has been described. The orthodox school still adheres largely to the idea that diseases are separate entities each requiring a specific remedy, even though the idea is gaining ground that the causes of diseases, particularly the chronic degenerative states, must generally be *multifactorial* (due to more than one cause). In either case, the doctor almost invariably resorts to the expedient of using drugs to suppress discomforting symptoms such as pain, fever, inflammation, accumulation of fluid, etc., and this is the general practice in regard to rheumatic disease. This is 'modern scientific medicine', relying largely on the products of chemotherapy, even though the latter may fail to relate to the causes of the complaints.

Such artificial, makeshift treatments might be regarded with a degree of indulgence were it not for a more sinister aspect of chemotherapy, namely that without exception every such medicine which is effective in the sense of suppressing one or more symptoms has in addition other effects than those for which it is prescribed. These, as already mentioned, are termed 'side-effects', a term which might appear to mean that these unwanted effects are relatively unimportant. On the contrary, they are in fact drug-induced diseases which are referred to in medical literature as *iatrogenic* diseases, a term which literally means 'doctor-induced' diseases. Sometimes they are called *DOMP*, standing for 'Diseases of Medical Practice'. Thus patients are likely to suffer from one or more drug-induced diseases in addition to their original disease.

These drug diseases, far from being trivial, are admittedly killing

59

thousands of people every year. It has been estimated that up to 15 per cent of patients occupying hospital beds are suffering from iatrogenic diseases. The dangers of drug effects were more fully realised following the thalidomide tragedy when a Committee on the Safety of Drugs was officially appointed with a doctor chairman, Sir Derrick Dunlop. It was thus realised that *every* effective drug was a poison, and the more 'effective' it was in suppressing symptoms the more serious were the side-effects. Sir Derrick Dunlop eventually stated that the known mortality and morbidity due to drugs was only 'the tip of the iceberg', and he complained that the chief difficulty of the Committee in identifying drug dangers arose because doctors were very largely failing to report such cases.

Drug Damage

A more recent estimate of drug damage appeared in January 1976 when medical authorities in the USA announced that medicines killed 30,000 each year *at a conservative estimate,* and that 'perhaps ten times as many patients suffer life-threatening and sometimes permanent side-effects such as kidney failure, mental depression, internal bleeding and loss of hearing and vision'. Similar problems of mortality and morbidity exist in Great Britain and every country where modern medical methods are practised. The standard reference volume for doctors is *The Side Effects of Drugs* (edited L. Meyler and A. Herxheimer). In the Preface the authors state: 'Drug-induced side-effects have been called diseases of medical progress... Since there are no active drugs without undesirable side actions, no toxicological experiments will ever be able to assure complete safety for their use in humans.' In prescribing them, doctors are said to take ' a calculated risk'.

It is well to realise that under the drug treatments of modern medicine sufferers from chronic degenerative diseases such as rheumatism are likely to deteriorate further until they are – if they survive – reduced to a state of morbidity which Dr Kenneth Vickery, Medical Officer of Health for Eastbourne, described as 'a state of medicated survival'. This sort of predicament is far removed from a state of health and well-being, and it is imposing ever-increasing burdens on both individuals and civilised society.

Among the worst features of drug treatment is that the side-effects of any drug are generally unknown when it is first made available, with accompanying manufacturer's sales-promotion literature. In most cases, four or five years of extensive use will have passed before harmful side-effects are identified. Aspirin was selling freely for over

60

half a century before it was identified as being the cause of internal bleeding, resulting in anaemia in many cases. Phenacetin was in use for a similar period before it was identified as a cause of destructive damage to the kidneys. Unfortunately, the drugs used in rheumatic cases invariably have side-effects, mostly severe.

The alternative school of natural healing is based on the study of the whole person and the identification of the natural causes of his diseases, particularly those relating to his habits and environment. Thus, according to Professor René Dubos, 'All medical faiths continue to proclaim allegiance to Hippocrates even though the Hippocratic Corpus, like the Bible, is often invoked but hardly ever read' (*Man Adapting*). Dubos also mentions that medical scientists 'can all trace their scientific ancestry to the Hippocratic teachings but otherwise their attitude and professional activities have little in common'. He adds that, as between these two schools of thought and practice, 'the debate has lasted 2,000 years'.

A School of Drugless Healing

Clearly, such a debate can be decided only on the basis of practical results. The beginnings of a new school of natural healing were introduced in the nineteenth century, as described in Chapter 4, by pioneers of hydrotherapy such as Priessnitz, Rikli, Schroth, Kuhne, Just, Kneipp and others. All these and others like them were aware that good nutrition was important, although there was no school of nutrition in their day. In spite of strong medical opposition, the new ideas of natural methods of treatment were not abandoned, even with the appearance of the germ theory, of which Dubos writes: 'There is no more spectacular phenomenon in the history of medicine than the rapidity with which the germ theory of disease became accepted by the medical profession.'

From that time onward the rift widened between the chemotherapy school and the methods of natural therapy which later became known as *nature cure*. From Central Europe it spread to the USA, where the leading exponents included Doctors Tilden, Caleb Jackson, Trall, Kellogg and others.

Caleb Jackson, given up by doctors as being incurable at the age of thirty-five, was treated by a pupil of Priessnitz. He recovered to found the Jackson Sanatorium for nature cure treatment, which became one of the greatest in the USA. When Jackson died at the age of eighty-five, in 1898, the sanatorium was taken over by the famous Bernarr Macfadden, who founded several magazines and wrote numerous books on natural health. He also founded a school for training

61

practitioners, of which one of the pupils was Stanley Lief, the pioneer of nature cure in England.

Also in the USA, Dr Andrew T. Still founded the first school of osteopathy in 1874. This gave new significance to the importance of the role of body mechanics and the nervous system in health and disease. Some twenty-five years later D. D. Palmer introduced the chiropractic techniques. Both of these systems are widely practised today.

Also in the USA, Dr Henry Lindlahr founded the Lindlahr Sanatorium, the largest of its type in America. He taught and expounded the theory that 'every acute disease is a healing effort of Nature', and maintained that the suppression of acute illness by drugs, serums and surgery was one of the most potent causes of chronic disease later on. His books, *The Philosophy of Nature Cure* and *The Practice of Nature Cure* became extensively used by students of these subjects.

Nature Cure in England and Scotland

Soon after the turn of the century nature cure was introduced into Great Britain. Bernarr Macfadden came to England and, in 1909, he opened a health sanatorium on the sea-front at Brighton. This was successful, but it was closed due to the outbreak of war in 1914. Macfadden returned to the USA, but in 1919 he came back to England with his pupil Stanley Lief and they opened a health home at Orchard Leigh on the Chilterns, where Lief took charge. A larger establishment was opened later which was to become internationally famous for its successful treatments, drawing patients from all sections of society – this was Champneys, at Tring, in Hertfordshire.

Meanwhile in 1913 Andrew Pitcairn-Knowles with his wife had established at Riposo Hydro, Hastings, a centre for the Schroth Cure, a combination of dietary treatment and hydrotherapy which he had learned in Dr Schroth's Sanatorium at Lindewiese in Austria; after his decease, in 1956, he was succeeded by his son, Gordon Pitcairn-Knowles, who died in 1963 – a few months before Riposo was to celebrate its fiftieth anniversary. The hydro was closed soon afterwards, even though the successful results of its treatments were then gaining wider recognition. In 1919, James C. Thomson, a member of Dr Lindlahr's staff in Chicago, returned to his native Scotland and founded the Edinburgh School of Natural Thera-peutics, which provided a four-year full-time course for students, including clinical experience.

After Macfadden's return to the USA, Stanley Lief continued his

62

excellent work and, in 1927, with John G. H. Wood, he founded the monthly magazine *Health for All,* which in 1976 was incorporated in the magazine *Here's Health.*

A small but dedicated group of medical practitioners who were vegetarians, having established their practice on humanitarian principles, united to found the Nature Cure Clinic in 1928 with premises in Ebury Street, Victoria, London. The Ebury Street premises were destroyed by enemy action in 1940 but the clinic was able to carry on in temporary premises in Dorset Square, London NW1. In 1946 the Clinic acquired premises in Oldbury Place, Baker Street, W1, where it still remains. Recently the premises have been rebuilt and expanded. With all these activities still continuing, very many thousands of people, including a large proportion of rheumatic sufferers, have experienced benefit by means of natural treatments directly related to the basic causes of their complaints. A large proportion of these cases had already been dismissed as 'incurable' by doctors and specialists of the modern orthodox school.

Thus for more than half a century a division in medical practice has existed and has grown wider: on the one hand medical orthodoxy has pursued the sophisticated path of chemotherapy treatment, while on the other a comparatively small but highly significant minority of doctors and naturopaths have practised and developed a practical expression of the teachings and principles of the Hippocratic tradition brought up to date in the twentieth century.

There is ample evidence to support the conviction that only by means of these drugless therapies will it be possible to overcome the great burden of chronic and supposedly incurable disease which now afflicts our civilised society.

The First Radio Debate

In a BBC radio debate in 1951 between Tom Moule, Secretary of the British Naturopathic Association*, and a Fellow of the Royal College of Surgeons the latter asked how a case of pneumonia would be treated under nature cure methods. Mr Moule replied that fasting and cold water compresses would be indicated in the acute phase, followed by strict regulations of the patient's dietary, but this view was dismissed by the doctor, who said that his professional colleagues would not consider this form of treatment as they could not expect their patients to alter their way of life, and he maintained that 'We have to treat them as they are.' Much the same idea still exists today in orthodox

*Now the British Naturopathic and Osteopathic Association.

63

medicine, where in most cases, the patient is expected to do no more than merely continue taking the tablets as prescribed.

Therein lies a basic distinction between the methods of the two schools. The failure to eradicate the *causes* of our maladies is largely responsible for the high incidence of chronic disease today, with so many sick people existing in a state of 'medical survival'; nor is this survival so lengthy, for the expectation of life at the age of fifty is very little greater than it was at the beginning of the century, in spite of the 'wonder drugs'.

CHAPTER 11

The Science and Art of Living

The body's intrinsic power of healing and repair heals our wounds, mends our broken bones and ensures that acute illnesses – colds, 'flus', catarrhal discharges and many other conditions – are self-limiting. *The 'incurable' chronic diseases of today result from our failure to deal effectively with the true causes of acute disease while 'fighting' to suppress the mechanisms of self-healing at a time when we should be doing everything possible to ensure the successful outcome of these vital curative processes.*

It should not be difficult to accept the fact that a simple solution to the problems of degenerative disease does not exist, nor is it likely that one will appear. This particularly applies to all the various forms of rheumatism.

It is important that this fact should be understood and accepted by those who try remedy after remedy in the vain hope that, at last, something will turn up which will do the trick. It is no more likely that such a panacea will be discovered by means of pharmaceutical research than that one will be found among the many and varied 'old wives' remedies to which so many sufferers still resort.

The ever-flowing torrent of pharmaceutical chemicals now manufactured and consumed bears little or no relationship to the attainment and maintenance of health and its corollary, the promotion of healing and repair. In this respect pharmacology, the study of drug treatment, must be, to use an academic term, the wrong 'discipline' as far as positive health is concerned.

The *true* science and art of living is more nearly dependent upon the principles expounded in Chapters 9 and 10, namely the seeking for and identification of the influences which threaten and disturb the essential balance of the many complex processes which Cannon termed 'homoeostasis', including the maintenance of the constant state of our vital fluids, blood and tissue fluid.

In addition, we need to identify and understand the nature and purpose of the processes by which the body responds in order to restore the normal state when such disturbances occur. Hippocrates,

65

having observed that many disease processes are self-limiting and self-curative, assumed the existence of an indwelling force which was termed the *Vis Medicatrix Naturae* (the natural healing force). The discoveries of modern physiology have done nothing to disprove this concept, although it now seems that instead of a single, specific *force* there is a health-oriented inborn wisdom of the body operating a programmed system of responses involving many processes which may all work together for the integrity of the individual.

Self-limiting Diseases

These natural healing processes are seen in their simplest form in cases of the common cold or influenza. Doctors are well aware that these are self-limiting illnesses and many GPs now wisely advise such patients to do nothing but rest and avoid chilling. They are becoming increasingly reluctant to prescribe drugs, although they may be aware that, as a result, many patients may be dismayed and may even consider that their case is being neglected. In cases of this kind the naturopath may assist the natural process of healing with drugless methods of treatment in order to ensure that recovery is more complete. In the more chronic and degenerative conditions of rheumatism and arthritis there is an even greater need to avoid the use of suppressive drugs to mask the painful symptoms and to employ drugless methods to assist the natural curative efforts of the body towards complete recovery.

From these observations it appears, first, that in the treatment of rheumatic diseases all the discernible causes should be identified as clearly as possible, both as regards our way of life and habits and also any causes which may arise from external environmental sources. Secondly, it follows that we should endeavour to eradicate or modify causative factors and, thirdly, that all positive assistance should be given to the healing and restorative powers which normally we all possess.

The Principal Causes of Disease

We must furthermore abandon the commonly held notion of 'fighting' nature, which has so greatly coloured medical and lay thinking. In its place we must substitute the principle of co-operation with the laws and powers of nature. We need essentially to give the maximum possible assistance to the body's natural processes of healing and repair. In place of the negative concept of a 'war against disease', we should take a more fruitful, realistic and positive line of thought and action – that of faithfully following the path to better health and assisting the very real and efficient protective and restorative powers which are the natural agencies upon which, in the final outcome, we are all completely dependent.

The principal factors in disease causation may be classified under three headings, namely:

1 faulty nutrition and elimination,
2 faulty body mechanics,
3 functional and, ultimately, structural impairment of vital processes resulting from negative mental-emotional states and
   behaviour.

The causes included under this classification predominate in almost all illnesses and particularly in rheumatic and other chronic degenerative diseases.

The degree to which any or all of these causes are involved in each individual will determine both diagnosis and treatment.

Group 1

In this group we must include not only what we consume in our daily dietary but also the total intake from our external environment.

It must be also understood that, useful as the threefold classification may be, there is also a constant relationship between one and another of these causative factors. For instance, oxygen may be regarded as being the number one food. We can live without it for only a matter of minutes, it is needed by every one of the many millions of living cells which compose our body, and it is essential to almost every biochemical reaction occurring in the course of our vital processes. Both the adequate intake of oxygen and the equally essential elimination of the body's gaseous wastes (mainly carbon dioxide) are, of course, dependent upon the mechanical process of breathing.

'We Are What We Eat'

The much repeated assertion 'We are what we eat' is obviously true in the physical sense that food supplies the materials from which all our tissues are built, maintained and repaired and that from our food we derive our physical energy and body heat. Thus, while it must be agreed that 'we eat to live', some people, unfortunately 'live to eat', meaning that they regard food and eating almost, if not entirely, as a

67

form of pleasure, dictated mainly by considerations of titillating the palate and with little or no regard for the primary reason for eating – nutrition.

Unfortunately, this attitude to food is encouraged by the fashionable catering establishments. Such overindulgence finally results in jaded tastes and appetites which are then stimulated with increasingly strong condiments and other flavourings.

Inevitably, a large proportion of those who thus 'live to eat' will, if they survive, join the ranks of those suffering from the progressive diseases of degeneration with malfunction of overladen organs – heart, liver, kidneys, etc. – and almost certainly from one or more forms of rheumatic disease with increasing incapacity. In many of these cases, following the failure of medication, the sufferer turns to the orthopaedic surgeon as a last resort for belated repairs and replacements of hopelessly damaged joints and other tissues.

At the other end of the social scale people also acquire dietary habits peculiar to their own fads and fancies, generally having a large preponderance of 'filling' foods in complete ignorance of the known principles of nutrition. These habits may have a hereditary influence inasmuch as the puddings which mother makes are like the puddings grandma made before her. The cafés and less fashionable restaurants in many cases have not altered their conventional dishes very much since the beginning of the twentieth century. Many of the dietaries of the 1890s and early 1900s, before the discovery of vitamins and the essential value of minerals, constituted what, in his book *The Englishman's Food,* Sir Jack Drummond, FRS, termed the 'English poverty disease, saying that it was inferior to the food of the peasant of the middle ages. This way of feeding in comparatively recent times mainly accounted for the fact that tuberculosis (then termed 'consumption') was a principal killer disease in the decades up to the First World War. Also, the bone-deforming disease of rickets was widespread in children throughout the formative years. These diets were sadly lacking in the fruits and vegetables which are the source of certain vitamins and essential mineral salts, and in the absence of these protective foods the body's defences were forced to develop the reaction of fever in an effort to restore the essential balance of homoeostasis (see p. 24). The fevers of those days inevitably raged fiercely and the mortality rate was high.

Dietary habits die hard, it seems, for large quantities of deficiency foods are eaten today – the supermarket shelves are largely laden with them – and individual resistance to any change of diet still persists in many people in spite of what has been referred to as the 'slimming craze'. Most of the deficiency foods are fattening and they also tend to

68

induce overeating, as if the instinct of the body is in this way seeking true satisfaction. As a result, the population as a whole is largely overweight.

Beware of the Danger Foods

Chief among the danger foods today are the refined carbohydrates which feature so largely in the civilised dietary. First, there is white flour in its many forms, including bread, cakes, biscuits, pastry and pastas – macaroni, spaghetti, etc – as well as white rice (often referred to as 'polished rice').

The old process of producing flour by stone-grinding allowed the whole grain with the wheatgerm and the bran to be included together with the white, starchy substance in order to produce wholemeal flour. The introduction of the modern steel-roller milling means that the bran and the germ are rejected so that much of the nutritionally rich parts of the whole grain are excluded from the flour and are then collected separately to be profitably sold – the bran as animal food or in packets as a breakfast food and the germ as a variety of special foods. The bran, once thought to be useless as human food or even harmfully indigestible, is now recognised as being very important for maintaining the healthy condition and functional efficiency of the intestine. In this modern process there is also loss of protein, valuable minerals and vitamins, especially those of the B-complex. Both natural iron and calcium are among the minerals which are lost, so by government decree iron is added to white flour in another form, as well as chalk to replace the absent calcium. In addition to this *mechanical* manipulation of flour, *chemical* manipulation takes place on a considerable scale. These mechanical and chemical treatments of food are often called 'the sophistication of foods'. It is stated that as many as twenty chemicals may be used in the production of the modern white loaf of bread. Such chemicals include bleaching agents (to make the flour whiter), preservatives, texturisers, anti-infection agents, emulsifiers, moisturising agents, anti-staling agents, etc.

In view of the loss of vitamins (especially those of the B-complex) the Ministry of Food issued directives that two commercially produced vitamins shall also be added to white flour – a process which is termed 'fortification' or 'enrichment'. Regarding this procedure, Sir Jack Drummond stated that 'this fails completely to answer the problem'. The reason for this was explained by E. W. McHenry in the *Canadian Public Health Journal* of September 1960, namely that members of the B-vitamin complex are only functional when present naturally with the remainder of the B group. He stated, 'There is no wisdom in removing eight or more needed vitamins and then adding only two to make good the loss.' *The British Medical Journal* of 26 January 1963 published experimental work which showed that there is no evidence that the 'fortification' of flour is of therapeutic value. Many people do not realise that in certain so-called 'brown' breads, some of which contain 75 per cent of white flour, chemical colouring agents are added.

In addition to the many chemicals which may be used in the making of white bread and some brown (but not wholemeal) breads, there is now a further risk of contamination of flour from the many chemicals used in agriculture.

During the Second World War the introduction of wholemeal or almost entirely wholemeal flour produced a marked improvement in health with a decrease in constipation and dental decay. After the war, a report to this effect from the Channel Islands concerning the period of German occupation was presented to the House of Lords. At the same time the millers and bakers in Britain were pressing for a complete return to the use of white flour on the assumption that the public wanted it. Also, no doubt, the bakers wished to ply their art in making the fancy cakes and pastries to which white flour lends itself. On the strength of the health report from the Channel Islands and elsewhere a directive was issued that wholemeal bread and flour should be made available according to demand.

White Sugar – the Foodless Food

The second 'rogue' food – possibly even more damaging – is white sugar, in all the various forms in which it appears. Sugar eating is a relatively recent innovation in the many millions of years of man's history and prehistory. At the time of Queen Elizabeth I the explorers and colonisers were bringing back cane sugar from the West Indies, and it was distributed among some of the wealthy, including Court circles. Pepys, in his diary, remarked on the 'blackened teeth' (tooth decay) of the aristocracy, who alone ate sugar. By the year 1700 the commercial refining of sugar had made it more available, to the point where, it is stated, the consumption of sugar had risen to about 4 lb per year per person. By 1800 the figure had risen again to about 16 lb per head. By 1900 consumption had risen again to about 80 lb per head, and at the present time it runs at about 120 – 130 lb per person per year.

Never before have humans been so exposed to this 'foodless' food, which possesses none of the advantages of natural foods in that it does not include any of the protective substances such as vitamins and

70

minerals. In fact, it induces an addictive tendency (its chemical formula closely resembles that of alcohol).

A decade or so ago the slogan was 'sugar for energy'. This sounded fine; 'that stuff' with the sweet taste being sold at so many shops in the form of 'sweeties' in all manner of shapes, sizes and colourings, will make us strong and energetic – just the thing to give to the kiddies as a reward for 'being good' or in larger fancy packs to please the girl friend or wife! The 'energiser' was also incorporated in many articles of everyday diet – puddings, pies, tarts, cakes, buns and biscuits and more things besides and this seemed to be just what we needed.

Now the story is different – little is heard about the slogan 'sugar for energy'. On the contrary, it is now recognised that the habitual consumption of refined carbohydrates, particularly white sugar, is the principal cause of dental caries (tooth decay). Moreover, the danger does not end there. It is realised also that the refined carbohydrates are a principal cause of some of the most prevalent diseases in our civilised community, including, in addition to dental decay, such diseases as obesity, diabetes, peptic ulcers, diseases of the intestine such as colitis and diverticulitis, and diseases of the blood-vessels such as varicose veins, haemorrhoids and constipation, all of which result from degenerative changes, of which rheumatic disease is a frequent manifestation.

In their book *Diabetes, Coronary Thrombosis and the Saccharine Disease*, Drs Cleave, Campbell and Painter, after listing the disorders which they term 'the saccharine disease', state:

> . . . it would be an extraordinary coincidence if these refined carbohydrates, which are known to wreak such havoc on the teeth, did not also have profound repercussions on other parts of the alimentary canal during their passage along it, and on other parts of the body after absorption from the canal. As an extension of this argument, we consider that the above list by no means includes all the manifestations of the saccharine disease, and that later workers will add to the list to an extent that would not be believed at the present time.

(The writers explain that the adjective 'saccharine' means 'pertaining to refined carbohydrates'.)

Diseases are not Entities

All this indicates the need to revise or abandon the lingering concept that diseases are *entities,* each requiring its own specific remedy, an

71

idea which for centuries has coloured the outlook both of the medical profession and of the general public.

Naturopaths (the practioners of natural healing), on the other hand, have long recognised that similar symptoms may be related to a variety of conditions, most or all of which may be manifestations of a basic ill health and degenerative process. This principle applies to most diseases and particularly to the chronic degenerative diseases, in which the orthodox medical methods of treatment have been so singularly unsuccessful. Moreover, such symptoms represent the natural healing and restorative efforts to counteract the state of generalised lowering of health. From this it follows that the general state of the body must be treated while specific measures are being taken to deal with the particular form of the disease. As noted in Chapter 2, there are numerous forms of rheumatism and without this broader approach to treatment any success can only be limited and partial at best, and in many cases the disease may worsen rather than improve.

The Principle of Wholeness

All this relates directly to the treatment of rheumatism and arthritis and it concerns particularly what may be regarded as the most important principle in nutrition – namely the principle of *wholeness*.

Foods in their natural state are a complex combination of substances, and in pure chemistry terms no single food is 'chemically pure'. If any one of these complex nutritional components is extracted, crystallised, washed and recrystallised until all other matter is removed, the end-product is, in chemical terms, a *pure substance,* although as a food it may be nutritionally valueless or even detrimental or dangerous. Unfortunately, in the modern processing of food, such operations are all too common for the well-being of the consumer.

Sugar provides an outstanding example of the above principle. It is well known that the native children in the West Indies regularly chew and eat the sugar cane, often in large amounts, without this causing dental decay or other troubles associated with eating white sugar. When the sugar is extracted from the cane and refined, the product becomes lighter in colour after each stage of refinement. This means that the darker sugar, such as Barbados, etc., still contains some nutrients which are absent in the final product, white sugar.

There are other similar examples which indicate that in the processing of natural foods the greater the degree of refinement and removal of natural constituents the greater is the possibility of loss of food value, until the residual concentrate may become nutritionally inferior or even harmful. Not infrequently the substances which are rejected in the refining process are just those parts of the whole-food complex which are protective to health and which ensure maximum nutritive value. It is a fact too that, in general, the orthodox medical outlook on nutrition is also largely fragmentary.

Directives to patients, if they are given at all, are almost always confined to the omission of one or other specific food, such as carbohydrate restriction in diabetes. Other nutritional factors are generally ignored.

Quite differently, in natural therapy, the principle of wholeness is particularly observed in the treatment of disease – both the acute and chronic forms – and most of all in treating chronic degenerative disease, the category which embraces the majority of rheumatic disorders. The threefold causative factors (see p. 67) will provide not only a basis of treatment but also the guidelines to healthy living.

Here it may be asked, 'What are the limits of natural methods as regards improvement and eventual cure?' The answer is that in the majority of cases improvement is well in excess of the sufferer's highest expectations, given reasonable patience and determined perseverance. The limitation of recovery depends on the amount of damage to vital organs and tissues which has already occurred, but even in many of the more severe and long-standing cases the methods here advocated may halt further deterioration and in many cases ease or banish pain and increase mobility.

First then, in the next chapter, we will deal with the nutritional factor.

CHAPTER 12

The Essential Therapy

The treatment of arthritis and other rheumatic ailments must be related to causes, and certain measures of self-help are mandatory if cure is to become a reality. The same rules also govern the problems of prevention.

The facts and explanations so far presented indicate that rheumatism and arthritis, both in their acute and chronic states, are due mainly to natural causes, many of which it is possible to identify. It follows that these disease conditions must be treated accordingly in relation to the total of these causes.

This realisation obliges us first to identify as completely as possible the causes, both general and particular, not overlooking personal factors arising from mistaken and faulty habits as a result of which, however unknowingly, we may have been transgressing the natural laws which govern our state of health or disease.

No Single Cause of Disease

It must be realised that seldom, if ever, is there a *single* cause for any one of the forms of rheumatic ailments. Among the many possible causes, those which may be classed as 'natural' are not difficult to define, and from this we can determine what should be done by way of treatment in order to remove or counteract these causes and their effects. Furthermore, we can then decide what are the necessary changes or modifications of faulty habits of life which may have interfered with the body's natural functions, distorting or suppressing the very vital processes which are continually striving to restore and preserve the state of natural health.

What may be regarded as natural causes of ill health are those factors which may be classified under the three main headings referred to on page 67. A similar classification would have applied in past centuries with comparatively minor differences. In some ways, there have been, over the years, a number of changes for the better, such as improved sanitation, water supplies, housing, etc., and a wider variety of available food, largely due to vastly improved transport facilities.

Supplies of whole, natural foods, many organically grown, are now becoming much more readily available.

Against these advantages, we are nowadays in a situation where, in addition to the natural, intrinsic causes of disease, modern industrialised communities are exposed to a large number of environmental health hazards which have arisen from the very rapid and in some cases irresponsible operations of modern industrial technology. This applies particularly to what has been termed the 'chemical explosion', whereby great quantities of hitherto unknown substances, many of which are very poisonous, have been projected into the environment. Very many chemicals are used in food processing and as additives.

Fortunately, there are numerous courses of action which we may adopt in order to restore and preserve the balance of health, and most of them are simple, logical, straightforward and potentially effective. Thus, we are not powerless to help ourselves to better health and, correspondingly, to greater freedom from disease.

The Choice is Yours

It is, however, essential to accept that we may not attain this desirable objective unless we are prepared to undertake certain necessary positive, practical measures of self-help. As a reward for these efforts, the increased vitality, capability and sense of well-being which will be gained are far removed from the morbid state of mere medicated survival which is the fate of so many today.

Rational as this may seem, long experience has confirmed that there are many who doubt the need to change a single long-standing habit, especially concerning ways of eating. A facile but fallacious and misleading argument that is often advanced is that some persons eat all the 'wrong things' without suffering from rheumatism. Surprisingly, there are those who use this and similar excuses to avoid undertaking a course of self-help. Rather than resort to such misleading devices to avoid taking necessary action, the rheumatic sufferer would be better advised to consider carefully the possible alternatives, namely:

1 To do nothing and to continue to suffer. This may appear to be foolish, but it may be partly explained by the fact that quite commonly a spontaneous easing of the rheumatic aches and pains takes place only for them to recur after an interval. These recurring remissions encourage the sufferer to hope that the condition may cure itself. He or she may also know that the doctors say there is no specific cure available.

2 The second alternative is to decide to seek or to continue with orthodox medical treatment.

The ostrich-like first of these options is likely to lead to further degenerative changes, worsening with each attack.

Regarding the second possible choice, the sufferer is likely to be told at some stage, 'No cure is available – learn to live with it.'

Then there are the 'first-timers' who, after attending the doctor, will depart (possibly after a brief examination, doctors being very short of time) bearing a prescription to the pharmacist for one or more drugs. The sufferer may do well to question this form of treatment, particularly if he is aware that an alternative drugless treatment exists, and also for the following reasons.

Rheumatic disorders are characterised by inflammation. Thus the doctor feels justified in prescribing his usual treatment with drugs which suppress inflammation, in this way treating the symptom and not the cause of the disease. He may also prescribe analgesic (pain-killing) drugs.

The medical profession has virtually excluded the possibility of asking the patient to alter his habits, particularly his habitual dietary.

Medical literature still asserts that there is no particular diet for rheumatic sufferers and few doctors ever go beyond advising an obese patient to reduce weight, generally without saying how this should be done.

The Dangers of Side-effects

What the doctor usually fails to mention is the fact that antirheumatic drugs are among the most dangerous with regard to side-effects and that they are likely to cause some form of iatrogenic (doctor-induced) disease.

Thus, among the anti-inflammatory drugs *phenylbutazone* (butazolidin) and its related compounds are known to cause nausea and vomiting as well as peptic ulceration with haemorrhage of the stomach and intestines (sometimes with perforation), skin rashes, sodium retention with oedema (swelling of the tissues due to fluid), and high blood pressure (hypertension). Even more serious are the effects of these drugs on the blood, with possible destruction of bone-marrow cells (the cells that make new blood), which may cause serious forms of anaemia.

Injections of *gold salts* may seriously damage the liver, kidneys and bone-marrow. There are similar pitfalls with other anti-inflammatory drugs and also with other drugs which are used to suppress the body's defensive mechanisms.

Among the worst are the *steriod* drugs *cortisone, prednisone, prednisolone, betamethazone* and others. Originally, the *cortis-*

costeroids, as these drugs are called collectively, were being hailed as great medical triumphs providing what at first appeared to be instant cures. This was in the 1950s, but the story is very different today. A decade later a panel discussion of medical specialists issued the following report regarding the treatment of rheumatoid arthritis:

We are very much more cautious about using steroids now, because once you start with them you may be stuck with them for life or for a very long time. A lot of patients we take into hospital are patients who have run into complications on account of steroids. They've got osteoporosis and vertebral collapse, or peptic ulcers, or various other things, and it is extraordinarily difficult to get them off.

Another doctor commented:

This is a problem of general practice. It is very difficult to maintain Olympian detachment when a patient with family commitments is suffering a good deal of pain and disability which can be relieved by steroids. In the past there has been a tremendous amount of pressure on general practitioners by patients themselves for these drugs. But it is interesting to note that during these last few months the pendulum is beginning to swing the other way, and I have actually had patients coming to me saying they didn't want to be put on steroids. People are beginning to realise the side-effects.

Although the steroids are effective in the suppression of symptoms, often to a dramatic extent, in the long run their effectiveness decreases so that many doctors consider that patients do as well or even better without them. Patients on steroids are given a steroid identity card and told to carry it at all times, owing to the development of a state of dependency when dangerous consequences may follow the sudden withdrawal of the drug, for example in accidental circumstances.

A further group of drugs has been introduced which are also termed *immunosuppressives.* They act to suppress the natural immunity reaction of the body which enables it to defend itself.

The drastic nature of such interference with a primary natural function is indicated by the fact that the use of these drugs is limited to very severe cases and the patient is kept under close observation with frequent blood-tests. Another drug with severe toxic side-effects is called *penicillamine* (not to be confused with penicillin). It does seem that many of the drugs which mimic, supplement, substitute or suppress the body's own natural biochemical substances, such as hormones, etc., are apt to exhibit the most undesirable side-effects, which are frequently morbid and sometimes fatal.

It is somewhat daunting to find that after a flood of new drugs there has been something of a return to older drugs, in particular *aspirin* and other related derivatives of salicylic acid which were first introduced in 1899. Aspirin, however, although it is less damaging than many modern drugs, can also be dangerous. Aspirin poisoning is stated to account for 15 per cent of all cases of overdosage. Persons sensitive to aspirin may suffer from vomiting, headache and high temperature. It may cause deafness, noises in the ears and, more recently, it has been proved to be the cause of severe irritation of the alimentary tract from stomach to colon, often causing internal bleeding and in some cases leading to anaemia from the constant blood loss. Also, it may cause gastric ulcer or diarrhoea. Unfortunately, when used to suppress rheumatic symptoms, it has to be prescribed in large doses daily, thus increasing the possibility of severe side-effects.

Another 'household remedy', *phenacetin,* has been largely withdrawn having been found to do severe damage to the kidneys, and there is no doubt that it has been the cause of much previously unsuspected morbidity and mortality by causing kidney failure.

Paracetamol has been produced as a substitute, but this drug has in turn been identified as a possible cause of liver damage. Most of these drugs may also adversely affect the central nervous system.

Natural Health or Medicated Survival?

It is not surprising that such artificial treatments lead, at best, to a state of 'medicated survival' that is far removed from the sense of well-being which accompanies natural health. Neither is it surprising that the National Health Service is showing signs of failure despite the enormous multimillion costs on the national budget. Modern scientific medicine has failed to solve the problems of chronic degenerative disease even after more than a century of chemotherapy. It is not hard to see the reasons for this failure, nor is there any indication that success in treating rheumatic disorders is likely to be achieved in the years to come by means of more and 'better' drugs.

On the other hand, the concentration on chemotherapy has established a multimillion-pound drug-manufacturing industry which is so great that its sudden collapse would precipitate an economic catastrophe. Moreover, this industry largely sponsors, influences or controls research organisations devoted to the search for more drugs, mostly produced by means of synthetic chemical techniques.

In this situation the role of the doctor, bombarded as he is with promotion literature couched in medical terminology and coupled with visits by the drug houses' representatives, is increasingly that of an intermediary between the drug manufacturer and the patient. It is very noticeable that doctors are reticent concerning their medicaments, and especially concerning the harmful and dangerous possible side-effects. Similarly, medical writers are uptight concerning the methods and results obtained by natural, drugless treatment, often making denigratory or facetious references to it as being 'cranky', whimsical or otherwise eccentric.

Doctors and Nature Cure

Unfortunately, few doctors have studied the results of these safe and effective drugless methods of natural treatment when they are thoroughly and persistently applied. Among the exceptions are certain doctors who are more receptively minded, such as the late Dr Bertrand Allinson, who was asked whether nature cure could perform miracles. He replied, 'instant miracles, no, but slow miracles, yes.'

Nowadays, there is a tendency to discount any idea or practice which may appear not to be 'scientific', and to assume that the answer to any and every problem will be provided by the host of laboratory technicians given sufficient time and – even more important – enough money for research. Technology, which is science related to industrial objectives, may be, and not infrequently is, found to be misapplied science, particularly when great amounts of international finance are involved. Such assumptions concerning scientific treatment may be dangerous.

Science is basically a search for truth. Historical records reveal that some of the most important truths are relatively simple and that many such principles have from time to time been lost sight of by becoming involved in ever-increasing diversity and complexity. What we are here concerned with – namely the living body's innate power to heal and maintain itself – is at its best when, and only when, its basic needs are observed and satisfied. *This is what nature cure is about.*

Long ago Hippocrates, with his great powers of observation, recognised the role of the body fluids with respect to health and disease. Although he was partially mistaken in his classification of fluids or 'humours', his theory was not replaced until well into the nineteenth century when Claude Bernard redefined the body fluids and their functions with what he termed the *milieu interne*.

Then it was realised that, in the simplest terms, the quality of life, as postulated by Rudolph Virchow, is determined by the integrity of the cell. To exemplify the ruling principle of the integrity of the cell and to illustrate this in simplest terms we may consider the amoeba – the simplest of all animal organisms, consisting of a microscopic single cell enclosed in an extremely thin membrane (Figure 5).

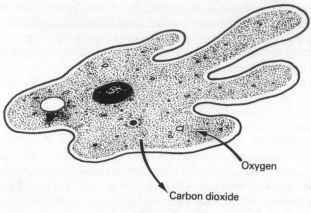

Oxygen

Carbon dioxide

5   The amoeba

The amoeba can move in its fluid environment and secures for itself a constant two-way flow through its membrane, whereby it breathes and thus receives a constant supply of oxygen and nutritional substances while discharging its waste materials, including carbon dioxide, into the surrounding fluid. Most of our cells, in contrast to the amoeba, are fixed so that the tissue fluid must circulate, thus constantly bathing the cells. This tissue fluid is filtered from the bloodstream and, as in the case of the amoeba, the two-way exchange of nutrients and wastes ensures continuity of function, repair of tissues, and cell replacement. As the human body develops from the foetus the cells differentiate and form colonies, so that liver cells are different from brain cells or muscle cells, etc., each type having its own properties and functions. This is one aspect of the basic life process which is termed *metabolism* and which includes the sum total of chemical changes in the living body.

The Fluid Transport System

A most remarkable property of cells is that they have the ability to respond to many forms of irritation and to react to such challenges with the process of *inflammation*. Such challenges may result from injury to tissues or from toxins in the blood or in the tissue fluid as it bathes the cell. *In healthy intact tissues, inflammation does not occur.*

Thus, it is clear that for the cells to maintain a condition of excellence and vital harmony the tissue fluid must be able to supply all the necessary nutritive materials which it should obtain from our food, via the alimentary tract, while simultaneously removing the cell debris and other unwanted substances (drugs, for example) to be excreted through the kidneys, lungs and skin. Therefore, the primary aim of treatment is to ensure that this fluid transport system is supplied with the right materials to meet the body's needs and to secure the necessary circulatory efficiency. This involves a primary principle of biology which is often sadly overlooked. There is one other concept which helps to define the causation of degenerative disease and form a scientific basis upon which to plan the treatment of rheumatic and other diseases. This is the concept of the role of *stress* as a factor in disease causation. In his book *The Stress of Life*, Professor Hans Selye, the Canadian physiologist, relates how the body's defence mechanism responds to the call for 'fight or flight', involving activity of the nervous system and the endocrine glands. Selye calls this the *alarm reaction*. If the body's mechanisms operate so as to meet the situation, all may be well and the threat to homoeostasis will be resolved. This Selye calls the *stage of resistance.*

If, however, the adaptive reaction is not able to maintain the pace of the response it will result in the *stage of exhaustion,* when illness begins to appear. Thus, Selye considered that in common with other degenerative diseases rheumatism and arthritis are diseases of *maladaptation to stress.*

Selye's concept is now generally accepted. There is therefore the need to define more precisely the factors of stress in each set of circumstances. In a recent scientific publication, *Health and the Environment,* to which a number of well-known scientists contributed, one of the contributors, Professor G. Melvin Howe, writes concerning present-day stressful factors: 'To define stress is difficult, but it may be recognised as comprising factors which act to disturb homoeostasis, impose a load on adaptable mechanisms, and likely to be manifest chronically, if not acutely, in a reduction in human fitness.' This expression may certainly apply to the rheumatic disorders.

For very many thousands of years man's adaptive powers have needed to respond to varying factors in his natural environment. He is now suddenly faced with the task of striving to adapt to new and unfamiliar changes, brought about mainly by human agencies, in his environment, both internal and external, and also with many changes of habits generally resulting from this new way of life. Modern civilised man is thus subject to stressful factors in ways he has never before experienced and to which so far he is not well adapted. Dr Howe points out that such stresses must be experienced at various levels – *biochemical, physiological* and *psychological*. These three levels of stress appear to be closely related to the three factors of disease causation (p. 67) which have long been adopted as a guide to naturopaths in the practice of natural therapeutics, and which thus appears to be strictly a scientific approach to the treatment of all rheumatic disorders.

It is essential to realise that rheumatic diseases invariably involve the whole body, with changes in the vital tissues, including the blood. These are indeed diseases of stress and maladaptation. Any treatment which does not rest upon these principles may not be regarded as being scientifically sound.

Part Two

Treatment

CHAPTER 13

Self-help the Natural Way

There exists a valid alternative to drug treatment – i.e. naturopathy, a treatment which provides both immediate and long-term measures to restore and maintain health.

The plan is explained in detail in the following chapters summarised for ease of reference in the appendix (pp. 222–5).

Having outlined in simple terms the conditions which the living body requires in order to maintain the balance of health and to restore it when it has become disturbed, a few more points need to be made before we present a detailed plan of treatment.

Professor Hans Selye has defined the disturbing factors which cause disease in terms of *stress*. This concept requires further consideration for the reason that stress is an essential factor in the lives of us all. Normally, various forms of stress serve to stimulate our latent powers by producing appropriate and adequate responses as, for example, the athlete who submits himself to stressful courses of preparation in order to increase his strength, skill or speed in performance. In such cases, successful adaptation will increase our resilience and capacity for work or play.

But if and when stress is excessive, cumulative or persistent and when, perhaps, involuntary forms of stress supervene, the adaptive mechanisms of the body may be weakened and over-taxed so that sooner or later maladaptation overtakes us, resulting in disease with increasing difficulty in maintaining homoeostasis.

It thus remains for us to define the factors of stress that are involved in rheumatic disorders. Professor Selye recognised that rheumatic disorders result from stress factors with which the defensive, healing and repair capacities of the body are unable to deal successfully. He stated: 'Rheumatic maladies are really typical diseases of adaptation, because if the body's defences are adequate the disease is suppressed without any intervention by the physician. These diseases are essentially due to inadequate adaptive reactions against comparatively innocuous injuries. They are due to maladaptation.'

Dealing with other Stress Factors

When Selye referred to the stresses which may cause these diseases as 'comparatively innocuous' he no doubt had in mind that rheumatic diseases are not 'killer diseases' and that, other than in the acute form of *rheumatic fever,* the onset is likely to be gradual with bouts of pain and stiffness which may vary in intensity from mild to severe and may resolve in a matter of days. This means that the body's natural healing processes have reacted to restore and, at least temporarily, to adapt.

But if the causes of the condition – the stress factors – are not in due course resolved, another bout, possibly more severe, will almost certainly supervene. Each succeeding attack is likely to result in some degree of degenerative change in the tissues involved, such as joint structures, muscles, connective tissues and possibly tendons and ligaments, accompanied by increasing disability and distress. Sooner or later the well-known signs of inflammation will appear in affected parts, with heat, swelling, pain, and possibly redness. With repeated bouts, a condition of sub-acute persistent inflammation may develop between more severe periods.

It should not be imagined that such states of rheumatism begin in an otherwise perfectly healthy body, although a localised condition of traumatic arthritis due to injury is the exception. In all cases of systemic rheumatism, prior disturbance of health will have occurred in one form or another. Such disturbances may include a history of catarrhal conditions, perhaps with colds, coughs, tonsillitis, sinusitis with involvement of the lymphatic glands, perhaps flu or other ailments, in some cases mild and in others more severe.

In other cases, and particularly with the middle-aged chronic sufferers from rheumatism, colds and other catarrhal states may tend to decrease while the rheumatic condition may be worsening. This may lead the sufferer to assert that 'Apart from my rheumatism, I'm a very healthy person. I used at one time to get colds, but now these occur very seldom.' This is a false assumption, as will be made clear in a later chapter. In fact it may prove to be a very dangerous one because some of the causative factors of rheumatism may also play an active part in causing other diseases, such as bronchitis, stomach and bowel disorders, heart diseases (possibly including coronary thrombosis), high blood pressure, varicose veins, etc., some of which may be fatal.

Whole-person Treatment is Vital

It should be realised, therefore, that the rheumatic sufferer is a sick person and that various aspects of the whole person may be affected. Likewise, if we neglect to resolve all the causative factors, and merely treat rheumatic complaints as if they are entities in themselves and not manifestations of disturbance of the whole body, the arthritis or other form of rheumatism may not only worsen but other symptoms will sooner or later appear because the principle of *whole-person* treatment has been neglected.

In general, the medical profession has not accepted this principle. Thus, it is quite usual to find doctors treating patients as having several separate troubles, regarding each as a single disease entity needing its own treatment, so that the patient may be having one prescription (tablets or injections, etc.) for inflammation, one for pain, another for accumulated fluid, and yet another for high blood pressure, all being taken at intervals throughout the day. In this now very common situation the doctor may find it practically impossible to identify which of the patient's symptoms are side-effects, which drug caused them and, still worse, which are due to one drug 'potentising' another, thus increasing the severity of its side-effects. In all such treatments it is certain that, to a greater or lesser extent, the patient will be suffering from one or other form of *iatrogenic* disease (see p. 59) in addition to a suppressed form of the original complaint. Is there any wonder that, however the forms of disease may change, the total amount of illness treated in this way is imposing an unreasonable burden on the whole of modern civilised communities?

Although some doctors are now thinking more about the need for self-help in health matters, in line with the principles of natural therapy, these doctors are unfortunately relatively few compared with the majority who show little or no signs of radical change in this direction.

Medical training and qualification in general tends to discourage any interest in the principle of *wholeness*. Also, the higher awards and higher echelons of the profession still belong largely to the specialists, whose studies mainly concern a particular disease or the ailments of a particular anatomical system. The psychiatrist may have little or no interest in or knowledge of body mechanics. The orthopaedic surgeon may have little or no interest in or knowledge of nutritional therapy, and so forth. Even the rheumatologist may be completely absorbed in his searches for artificial immunity or suppressives of pain and inflammation. The former, which involves the suppression of the body's natural defences, may well prove to be the most damaging and dangerous of all.

In this situation, the wisest course for the sufferer from rheumatism and arthritis to take is one of self-help, using as a detailed guide the following programme of practical treatment. These methods of natural therapy are the safest, surest and most effective form of

87

treatment for these ailments, providing in addition what may be called a bonus in terms of steadily increasing health, vitality and a sense of well-being. The successes achieved should not cause surprise because in both its theory and its practice *nature cure* (some prefer to call it *naturopathy* or *natural therapy*) is based on fundamental principles of biochemistry, physiology and pathology. It rests on the firm basis of natural sciences; it is sound common sense and readily comprehensible. Thus the use by Dr Bertrand Allinson of the word 'miracle' (p. 79) was not intended to indicate some form of supernatural intervention but that nature cure provides a supreme example of the effectiveness of the application of natural laws and processes to the problems of disease.

Many thousands have followed this path to health and have found their lives enriched and their physical powers increased, so as to become living examples of the excellence of mind and body which may be achieved by following these principles and practices.

The Essential Programme

It is, of course, necessary to emphasise that to achieve these benefits the programme of treatment must be adopted and followed *as a whole* and carried out thoroughly and persistently.

Almost a century ago the principle of wholeness was being emphasised by the exponents of nature cure, mostly failing, unfortunately, to gain general acceptance. Quite recently, however, we hear increasingly about *whole foods* and even orthodox medical writers are beginning to introduce the concept of whole-person treatment – a principle that is long overdue for recognition. The principle of wholeness may be expressed in the following terms: *'The whole is greater than the sum of the parts.'* An obvious example in the realm of mechanics is that the separate parts of a motor car take on a different quality when integrated by being assembled in the right order and, when supplied with the right fuel, they will have acquired the properties of a modern marvel of transport.

In the realm of biology the principle of wholeness is supremely significant. In fact health may be expressed as being a state of wholeness. To express this principle General Smuts coined the word *Holism,* meaning that the fundamental principle of the universe is the creation of *wholes,* particularly concerning the processes of life and mind. Any scheme of treatment which ignores or rejects this fact may not be expected to provide more than the temporary relief of symptoms. Only the well integrated, spontaneous self-curative power of the living body may serve to preserve the reputation of the physician.

88

To assist and secure the success of these natural curative processes as a whole is the principal aim of natural therapy.

In his exposition of the principle of the role of stress, Professor Hans Selye, does not seem to indicate whether or not he recognises that faulty nutrition is, in one way and another, one of the most potent factors of disease-causing stresses in our Western civilisation, affecting the biochemical integrity of the whole body. In this first category of the *Triad of Disease Causation* (see pp. 66–8) we must include the effects of any foreign substances, pollutants, etc., which we may ingest. The nutritional programme which follows is also calculated to promote and assist elimination of toxic wastes, the *accumulation of which is a characteristic feature of rheumatic disease.* It is prescribed according to the well tested principles of diet reform with emphasis on a balanced intake of whole, natural foods, thus providing much-needed vitamins, mineral salts and other essential factors all in proportionate amounts and in their natural context.

Such a dietary programme, in contrast with the many crash diets, relieves the constant stresses imposed upon the continuously active mechanisms of homoeostatic balance upon which health and life are dependent. It is, therefore, an essential basis upon which to build optimum health and vitality.

CHAPTER 14

Stage 1: Eliminating, Cleansing, and Revitalising

In this chapter the necessary measures of nutritional therapy are explained, and some possible difficulties and objections are shown to be fallacious.

The reader will do well to keep these points in mind when commencing Stage 2 of the Nutritional Therapy Plan (pp. 95-7).

Many people appear to have a deeply ingrained resistance to change, most of all in regard to their eating habits. Fortunately, the numbers of those who take such a rigid attitude are diminishing, while the numbers of those who find the idea of change more acceptable are increasing and many others are genuinely seeking help and advice concerning their dietary.

To the more reluctant ones – especially those suffering from the pains and limitations imposed by rheumatic disorders – it may truly be said that to free oneself from the slavery of harmful habits of eating is much less difficult than might be imagined. In response to a suggested change of dietary habit some will say, 'Oh, but I *enjoy* my food!' To these who thus wrongly assume that a beneficial change of habit must be distasteful, it is true to say that those who follow the plan as proposed will find, almost without exception, that within a matter of weeks their tastes, their likes and dislikes are beginning to change and that not only will they be enjoying their food and finding it satisfying but they will also experience a greater enjoyment of life as and when the burden of ill health begins to lift.

The proposed plan is set out in stages. The first stage is calculated to promote and assist the elimination of toxic wastes, the accumulation of which in the living tissues is a characteristic feature of rheumatic diseases, and also to relieve the body of excess fluid, which is a prominent feature in many cases.

Why Count Calories?

Many may be pleased to observe that this plan of nutritional therapy does not involve the somewhat burdensome necessity for calorie counting which, it should be stressed, may be no disadvantage as regards the true nutritional value of a dietary. The calorie is a unit of heat obtained by burning the item of food in a piece of laboratory apparatus (the calorimeter), thus treating food purely as a laboratory material. The calorie (the heat required to raise the temperature of a kilogram of water one degree centigrade) bears little or no relationship to the positive health effects of food and may not even directly relate to the available energy produced as a result of the extremely numerous and complex biochemical reactions taking place simultaneously in the living organism.

As already mentioned, obesity (excess weight) has long been recognised as a health hazard, but only recently has the full extent of its dangers been recognised (see p. 71), in particular when the excess 'calories' have been obtained from the refined carbohydrate foods – white sugar and white flour products. While not being a slimming diet in the popular sense of the term, the natural therapy diet plan is more realistic, perfectly safe and, in the long term, more effective than almost all the calorie-counting slimming diets. Count your calories if you wish; you will find that Stage 1 of the plan is well within your calorie count while Stage 2 has a relatively low calorie count. Just don't eat between meals or nibble.

There is a very good reason for this, which should be understood, namely that the whole-food plan is a plan for *health*. A recent survey indicates that 97 per cent of people on slimming diets were back to their original weight condition in about one year after completing their slimming diet. This shows the fallacy of the crash-diet approach to the problems of slimming, which, if wrongly planned, may be detrimental to health and even dangerous. A further mistake arising from pandering to the desire to lose weight rapidly is the implication that the process is going to be unpleasant, thus engendering the 'get it over quickly' idea on the assumption that the quicker the loss of weight the sooner will it be possible to return to a 'normal' diet. Almost inevitably this is followed by an increase in weight once more. After a certain interval a second period of crash-dieting may be embarked upon and weight may drop, only to rise again. Repetition of this experience has been referred to as the 'yo-yo' plan, in which weight alternates up and down instead of remaining constant. The 'slimmer' may eventually give up trying.

It should be readily understood that such a sequence of events will impose severe stresses on the body's metabolism, which may fail to achieve a satisfactory steady state of adaptation at any stage.

Another pitfall frequently encountered is the selection of a target solely in terms of weight. Since the 1950s doctors, largely as a result of having been alerted by the publication of life statistics compiled by the life assurance societies, came to regard obesity as a disease and thus began to advise their overweight patients to reduce. The patients usually ask how much weight they should lose, and in reply the doctor will usually hazard a guess which may be well off the mark in terms of health, being more often too little than too much. It is, in fact, difficult to guess a person's 'weight for health' due to differences in build, bone and muscle structure, etc., which may vary greatly even among people of the same height and age group.

Your Weight for Health

This matter of weight for health is more important than might be supposed, the reason being that, if weight reduction by a course of slimming dietary (the doctor rarely gives detailed instruction in this respect) proves to be substantially less than the total encumbrance of the tissues by excess weight, it is unlikely that the weight will remain constant at that figure. On the other hand, the weight of an overweight person may be expected as a result of following the natural therapy plan to decrease surely but steadily until it reaches the *weight for health* of the person concerned, at which figure, almost invariably, it will become stable with only minor day-to-day fluctuations, up or down, from this very significant figure. This fact does not appear to be widely recognised, although it may be demonstrated in the great majority of cases where this scheme is followed. There are, of course, valid reasons for this as with all natural phenomena. In this matter it is reasonable to assume that the relatively lethargic metabolism of the overweight person becomes stimulated into a more dynamic and efficient state of activity so that the factors maintaining homoeo-static balance of the system are less under stress and thus more effective.

In other words, when a person achieves the desirable state of positive natural health the scales will indicate the correct *weight for health,* which may differ quite considerably from a previous guesswork figure. In the same connection there are two further facts to be understood. First, the person who sheds only a portion of excess weight will find such a 'half-reduced' stage difficult to maintain. As so often happens, such a person may be heard to utter a remark such as, 'I only have to eat one cream cake and my weight goes up.'

The second fact, no less important, concerns those who are underweight. Many such people may say, 'However much I eat I can't put on weight.' It is a fact that in many such cases, although having

92

perhaps on medical advice eaten more of the fattening high-calorie foods, probably including the 'rogue foods' made of white flour and sugar – the refined carbohydrates – they may still not have succeeded in gaining weight.

Much to their surprise the majority of these underweight people will benefit from a dietary that is not very unlike that which is effective in reducing the obese person's weight. The underweight person should also understand that he or she may need to experience a further small weight loss during the eliminating and cleansing stage of the plan. Any such small loss will consist mainly of the toxic encumbrance which may have been the factor which has prevented a normal gain and steady maintenance of weight. This small but important initial loss should come to a halt and be followed by a gain in weight which will be small and gradual until the weight stabilises at what, for the person concerned, will be his or her *weight for health*.

Following this, on a balanced whole-food plan, such persons should be gradually enabled to engage in correspondingly increased physical activity with improving health and, in the case of the rheumatic sufferer, decreasing pain and stiffness. For those who are not severely incapacitated, any further increase in weight should be that which results from the building of healthy new tissue, mainly consisting of muscle development.

Do You Suffer from False Hunger?

There certainly will be a number of other causative stress factors in the many forms of rheumatism and arthritis, some due to faulty body mechanics and others arising from negative emotional states, all of which we may seek to resolve. This undertaking will be simplified and aided when the beneficial action of the programme of nutritional therapy is thoroughly understood and adopted. Mention has been made of the enjoyment of food, which should be natural and highly desirable.

Without a healthy appetite most people would neglect to eat, with disastrous consequences. There is, however, a further matter which calls for explanation, namely the fear of hunger, concerning which there have arisen a great many false notions, causing much confusion. The reason for this is that most people fail to distinguish true hunger from *false hunger*. Thus it may be seen that often those who eat most frequently and who have large meals are the first to complain of feeling hungry, particularly if a meal is delayed only an hour or so beyond the usual time. They may complain of feeling weak or faint for want of food. This is false hunger at its worst.

93

Such feelings as these are reactions of the nervous system which may be greatly increased by emotional tensions due to sub-conscious fears and alarms associated with ideas of starvation. Also, many people do not understand that we do not get energy and strength from the meal we have just eaten. Food has to remain in the alimentary tract (stomach and intestine) for some hours before it can be absorbed into the blood-vessels and transported to the liver and other organs. It then has to undergo many more processes prior to being transported to all the various tissues and organs (see pp. 120–1). This means that energy must be expended in the various stages of digestion, absorption and metabolism before the food releases its available biochemical energy to serve our physical activities along with other nutritional needs.

Even more significant as regards false hunger is the fact that, during a complete fast, sensations of hunger are felt only for a very few days. After four or at most five days without food, and with only water to drink, these sensations almost invariably disappear and the stomach and intestine settle down into a state of comparatively inactive rest.

In addition to understanding the significance of false hunger it should be realised that fasting is not the same thing as starvation. Starvation is possible and indeed it not uncommonly occurs while eating regularly but failing to supply certain essential nutrients, while perhaps overloading the system with what may be termed 'foodless foods' such as the refined carbohydrates. As a result, even members of wealthy families, perhaps with overindulged children, may be suffering from malnutrition and thus 'starving in the midst of plenty'. Examples occur, of course, at the other end of the social scale where dietary deficiencies are found in the poorer countries of the world.

Different again is the so-called 'hunger strike', usually undertaken as a form of protest for some or other political ends, and usually accompanied by intense, exhausting emotional overtones. This is, of course, true starvation in which force-feeding may worsen the situation.

The Controlled Fast

Quite differently, a controlled fast may be beneficial to both mind and body. Fasting was used as a treatment by Hippocrates and by many religious leaders, including Moses, Mahomet, Buddha and Christ, for the physical, mental and spiritual welfare of the sick. In modern times, fasting has been effectively employed by the leaders of the nature cure school, including Doctors Lindlahr, Shelton, Earl Livingstone, Stanley Lief and James C. Thomson of Edinburgh, and many others. Certain forms of fasts, usually short, are included in the treatments of nature-cure health hydros and in the now fashionable health farms. In his book, *Man the Unknown,* Professor Alexis Carrel states: 'In primitive life men were subject to long periods of fasting . . . all religions have insisted upon the necessity of fasting . . . fasting purifies and profoundly modifies our tissues.'

Having distinguished between fasting and starvation, it should be stressed that although fasting may be of great value in the right circumstances, such a procedure is not recommended in the first stage of the nutritional plan for the treatment of arthritis and other rheumatic diseases. The reason for this is that, in addition to food, the civilised person of today will take into his or her body chemical pollutants from many environmental sources. Moreover, it is certain that a large proportion of rheumatic sufferers will have taken, and perhaps are still taking, drugs (prescribed or otherwise), all of which are poisons and which have harmful side-effects; they may also complicate the effects of fasting in this early stage of treatment.

The Nutritional Plan   Stage 1

The following plan should be followed without additions or omissions.

First Two Days

Take only fresh, ripe raw grapes and melon, preferably four or five ounces of each at the usual meal times. No drinks should be taken during these days, because the fruits will supply water in its best form. The grapes should be well washed but not skinned.

It may be found that the amount of urine passed during these days is more than might be expected. This is because the fruits have a natural diuretic action. In contrast with the diuretics so frequently prescribed by doctors, the method of reducing surplus fluid with these fruits is wholly beneficial.

For the Next Seven Days

On Rising: A small tumbler of equal parts carrot juice and pure fruit juice, selecting from apple, grape or pineapple, but *not* the acid citrus fruits and juices – orange or grapefruit. These latter should be omitted and introduced at a later stage in limited amounts. (Pure unsweetened fruit juices are obtainable from health food stores. Carrot juice, for those who have not a juice extractor, may be freshly prepared by passing raw carrots through a very fine grater on to about four thicknesses of muslin through which the juice is then squeezed.)

Breakfast: Ripe raw fruit, selecting from apple, pear, grapes, melon, peach or pineapple as available (not more than two kinds of fruit at each meal).

Mid-morning: Mix a teaspoon of a yeast and vegetable extract into a cup of hot water. Drink hot or cold as preferred. (If possible select an extract such as Barmene or Tastex containing vitamin B_{12}, obtainable from health food stores.)

Mid-day Meal: Select a raw salad from three of the following ingredients: Shredded raw white-heart ('Dutch') cabbage or lettuce in season, or 'Chinese leaves' when available, watercress, shredded raw red cabbage, celery, grated raw carrot, grated raw beetroot, grated raw swede or parsnip, ripe tomato (in season), onion or leek (cut into thin rounds), cucumber with skin, parsley, endive or chicory, sliced green or red peppers. Immediately on cutting or grating the salad it should be sealed by mixing it in the dressing and thus preventing oxidation of vitamin C and other food factors.

As a dressing for salads use either a mixture of vegetable oil and lemon juice or cider vinegar, or yogurt mixed with some chopped chives, mint or parsley, adding a little honey if liked.

With the salad take a portion of cottage cheese.

Follow with ripe, raw fruit or fruit salad, selecting from the breakfast list as specified. (To the fruit salad a little cream may be added, but no sugar.)

Evening Meal: Ripe raw fruit selected as for previous meals. Follow with yogurt, stirring a small dessert spoon of molasses into about $\frac{1}{2}$ pint of yogurt. Please note that drinks should be limited to those listed previously.

This first stage of the nutritional plan will provide an alkaline residue on absorption, thus helping to reduce the condition of relative acidosis that is so generally present in rheumatic sufferers, also raising pH towards a better homoeostatic balance, while also providing much-needed minerals and vitamins. Moreover, if this first stage of treatment has been followed strictly it should already be possible at least to begin to reduce the dosage of any drug or drugs which are being taken.

If any joint or joints are inflamed or are particularly painful at this stage, the use of hydrotherapy, as described in Chapter 20, almost invariably gives relief which is safe and beneficial and is not just symptom-suppressive as is the case with drugs.

The second stage of the nutritional plan which must be followed immediately is given in detail in the next chapter.

CHAPTER 15

Stages 2 and 3:
The Whole-food Plan

Possible reactions to Stage 1 of the treatment are considered and the importance of correctly interpreting them is emphasised.

Problems of weight control are considered and the fallacy of the bland diet *is explained, as is the principle of* wholeness *in nutrition as it affects the body's capacity for healing and repair.*

The important role of the reactions of fever and inflammation is defined.

At this juncture it may be necessary and helpful to explain or clarify certain further points. It is probably true to say that in no other area of knowledge are there more misconceptions and prejudices than in the relationship of nutrition to health. This is particularly evident in regard to the subject of weight control.

At the conclusion of the First Stage, the nine-day plan presented in detail in Chapter 14, those who are obviously overweight are likely to have lost some of the excess tissue, perhaps 3–5 lb in some cases and 6–8 lb or even as much as 10 lb in others.

Among those who are substantially overweight there may be some who will have shed little, or even none, of their superfluous weight in this early stage of treatment. It is essential for these persons to understand that this plan is not intended to be a 'quick-slimming' scheme. Its aim is to eliminate such toxic wastes as may be present while improving the quality of normal tissue. Weight reduction may at first be delayed. On the other hand, there may be those who have not followed the planned programme strictly, having selected certain items only and saying, 'I'm getting round to it gradually.' They may be still looking for the wonder food which does not exist, having failed to realise how much the principle of wholeness dominates the subject of nutritional therapy.

Under-active Glands

Secondly, there are some people in whom there is a reduction in the

98

rate of biochemical activity – the metabolic rate – due to under-activity of certain glands, in particular the thyroid gland (see pp. 44, 50). In this way considerable stress is imposed upon the balance of homoeostasis. In an advanced form this may result in the condition known as *myxoedema,* a term meaning mucous swelling. Even a slightly lowered rate of metabolism will often delay the effect of the nutritional programme in reducing excess weight. Realising this, the person concerned should not be discouraged and should not conclude that in his or her case the treatment will be ineffective. On the contrary, it is the treatment which will provide the numerous nutritional factors such as minerals and vitamins which may be needed to restore the 'lazy' metabolism to normal activity, with a necessary, but possibly slow, reduction of excess weight. There will also be other ways in which improvement may be observed, including better general health and increased vitality, all of which may become apparent during or soon after the Second Stage. These advantages may also include the first signs of easing of the painful rheumatic symptoms.

Thirdly, there are those who are consistently underweight, even in the absence of any signs of wasting disease. These persons, as mentioned in Chapter 14, may have found that well-meaning advice to eat more fattening foods has been of no avail, particularly when the refined carbohydrates have been considerably increased. By following the whole-food nutritional plan these persons may expect at first some further initial weight loss (perhaps up to 3–4 lb – rarely more). This should not give cause for anxiety if it is understood that these small initial losses are evidence of the cleansing and eliminative processes performed by the nutritional programme, which subsequently will bring about a gradual increase in weight to what it should be for health, having shed toxic wastes which may prove to have been responsible for impeding previous efforts to gain weight. Thus, as with those in the other two groups, the underweight person should carry out the full plan of the First Stage of treatment and follow immediately with the Second Stage, just as detailed later. Then, with only minor additions to their dietary, they may be pleasantly surprised to experience a slow but comparatively steady increase in weight towards what should be their normal weight for health in accordance with their build and physique. If these processes appear to be somewhat slow, patience is essential. It should be remembered that in most natural processes there are limiting time factors and that in this way the eventual weight increase will consist of healthy tissue, which will be of lasting benefit in a number of ways.

Muscle Wasting

A further fact to be considered is that many forms of rheumatism are liable to cause wasting of the muscles, mainly due to lack of use because of pain. On the other hand, when 'pain-killers' and anti-inflammatory drugs are taken, the suppression of pain may tend to encourage overuse of joints and muscles, whereas pain, if not suppressed, would limit any use and movement which might at that stage cause further tissue damage. This could apply in regard to the corticosteroids and other drugs which are now in common use. This would also apply to the very large doses of aspirin still frequently prescribed in cases of rheumatic disease, and particularly in rheumatoid arthritis.

How this and other problems of pain may be eased and overcome with the use of natural therapy will be considered later in this book. (Refer also to the Summary of Treatment on p. 178).

Before presenting the Second Stage of nutritional therapy, there are certain other points to be mentioned which should also help the reader to understand the basis of natural treatment with its emphasis on the need for self-help. It has already been observed that rheumatic diseases are primarily stress disorders. This principle applies in varying degrees to a majority of diseases, and every organ of the body may suffer from functional disturbances. These, in turn, may lead to more deep-seated organic disease resulting from excessive or prolonged forms of stress, and in this respect no organ is more susceptible than the digestive tract.

Among those who suffer from rheumatic complaints there are many who have also experienced one or other of the various stomach or bowel disorders, possibly inflammatory diseases such as gastritis, peptic or duodenal ulcer, diverticulitis, or some other alimentary-tract disease. In such disorders doctors have been accustomed to insist on the patient adhering to what is known as a 'bland diet' in the belief that any form of roughage in food must irritate the sensitive membranes which line the interior of the digestive tract. Thus, with the bland diet, all foods containing roughage are excluded, and instead the refined carbohydrates – white bread, polished rice, etc. – are approved. Unfortunately these are the very foods which I have described as the 'rogue foods' and which are now identified as the main cause of a number of serious diseases (see p. 71). Also, all but the softest of vegetables are excluded from the bland diet, no skins or peels are eaten and raw salads are strictly forbidden.

There must be very many sufferers who are still strictly following some sort of bland diet on medical advice and so a brief explanation is necessary as to why this unnatural dietary is harmful even for the condition for which it is prescribed.

The Saccharine Disease

Naturopaths have always opposed this bland-diet theory and for many years they have successfully treated inflammatory conditions of the stomach and bowel with the judicious use of natural whole foods, which provide both bulk and a normal content of dietary fibre. Support for this naturopathic practice has been forthcoming in recent years from various medical authorities based on important statistical findings. The work of Sir Robert McCarrison and Dr Weston Price which was referred to in Chapter 9 has been followed with further statistics presented by Drs Cleave, Campbell and Painter (see pp. 70–1) and more recently by Dr Cleave in his book *The Saccharine Disease*. Further support has been produced by Professor D. P. Burkitt, MD, FRS, of the Medical Research Council, arising from comparative studies of native Africans living on their traditional diets and members of the same races who have lived in modern civilised communities on sophisticated foods. The second group are found to suffer from diseases characteristic of our civilisation which were hitherto unknown among their more primitive-living counterparts, diseases which respond only to a return to more natural foods containing, among other factors, bulk and roughage (fibre).

The Bland-Diet Fallacy

This recognition of the fallacy of the bland diet and of the importance of dietary fibre must be regarded by the medical profession as an important step forward towards better nutrition. As a result, in seeking a simple remedy, some doctors are advising patients to eat somewhat large quantities of natural roughage in the form of bran, to the extent that Professor Burkitt has been referred to as 'The Bran Man' (*Medical News,* 8 January 1973).

Certainly, this has led to considerable improvement in many cases of diverticulitis, colitis and other disorders of the alimentary tract, including constipation. But the mere addition of bran to an otherwise conventional diet can provide only a partial solution to the many problems of these and other diseases which are due to similar causes. In other words, the advantages of a balanced dietary, consisting of whole natural foods, greatly outweigh the advantages obtained solely by the addition of bran to an otherwise conventional diet. Such a balanced dietary will contain, besides bran, numerous other valuable forms of vegetable roughage in association with a balanced intake of the essential minerals, vitamins, enzymes and other food factors, known and unknown. These are the requirements for the highest possible state of health, and they are particularly necessary for

101

overcoming both the acute forms of rheumatism and arthritis and the more deep-seated and established chronic forms of these diseases.

It is possible that Professor Burkitt and other doctors interested in the relationship of nutrition to health would agree in principle with the above statement. It is also possible that, in formulating the 'Bran Plan', Professor Burkitt is mindful of the overworked GP who may possibly find time to prescribe the daily portion of bran but may not have time or even perhaps the inclination to go more fully into the practicalities of dietary reform and other essentials of healthy living.

Meanwhile, for very many people the present-day conventional dietary, including the bland diet, will continue to be a major cause of disease of the alimentary tract. All too frequently this leads to surgery for removal of all or part of the stomach, or parts of the intestine, and so forth. Such operations represent failure to cure or prevent these diseases, among which cancer is now all too common. Bearing in mind the principle of wholeness, it is easy to understand that the processes taking place in the alimentary tract are directly related to the metabolism of the whole body, affecting both general health and specific diseases.

The Primary Requirement for Health

Therefore, the primary requisite for health is that the alimentary tract *must* be supplied with food which contains all the necessary nutrients, including bulk and roughage. Moreover, the stomach and intestines must be healthy and efficient to perform the specific tasks of digesting and processing the foods into a form in which the nutrient factors are ready for absorption into the bloodstream to serve the needs of every living cell of the body.

Consequently, unless these conditions are fulfilled by making the necessary changes in our civilised way of life, particularly our eating habits, the already high incidence of chronic degenerative diseases, chief among which are rheumatism and arthritis, will continue to rise. Clearly, the adoption of a plan of whole-food nutrition is essential if we are to break the vicious circle of degenerative disease with resulting benefit to the whole body, including the health and efficiency of the alimentary tract itself.

These facts explain why it is that great sums of money and effort spent in laboratory researches have produced nothing better than palliatives. To use the word 'cure' in this sense is quite unrealistic. There is, however, a true and meaningful sense in which the word 'cure' may be used. The inborn, intrinsic capacity for healing and repair, namely the *Vis Medicatrix Naturae* observed by Hippocrates, is

102

nowadays expressed as nature cure (see Chapters 11 and 12).

This embraces the complex but highly efficient hereditary biological mechanisms which actively maintain the homoeostatic balance within permissible limits.

Doctors learn about this process in their medical schools. They know that, although they may stitch a wound or manipulate the ends of broken bone together, it is the body's own natural curative responses which heal the wound and mend the broken bone. These inborn healing and curative powers are also to be observed in what are termed 'self-limiting' diseases, from colds and influenzas to many more severe acute inflammatory and feverish illnesses. In all of these the associated inflammation and/or fever are signs of the curative effort, and as recovery proceeds the inflammation subsides and the temperature reverts to normal. It is only when these intrinsic curative powers are permitted, and perhaps assisted by natural means, to function fully, unhindered and successfully, that the word 'cure' may justifiably be used.

Natural Cure Underestimated

Unfortunately, doctors generally tend to underestimate the effectiveness of these natural processes. While appreciating that reactions of inflammation and fever have a 'good intention', all too frequently they mount an attack on the signs of the healing process, usually with a drug selected from the vast array of preparations actively promoted by the drug manufacturers. This practice continues (often with the excuse that the patient expects or even demands drug prescription) in spite of the fact that GPs and other doctors have been advised in recent years by higher medical authorities not to prescribe antibiotics and other drugs for conditions such as colds, influenza and similar self-limiting forms of illness. So-called 'wonder drugs' have been publicised to the extent that today's doctor may be considered negligent if he fails to prescribe them, even though, perhaps, he may do so against his better judgement.

In any event, the doctor will seldom explain to his patients the natural healing processes as a result of which most illnesses are self-limiting, and so the patient fails to realise that a policy of 'intelligent leaving alone' may be much better than medical interference, which may be positively harmful. It is unlikely that the patient will be told what he or she may do to assist the spontaneous natural curative processes, and even more rarely will the doctor explain what should be done to remove completely the causes of the illness.

In this manner, more especially with drug treatment and its

accompanying side-effects, recurrence may be expected sooner or later. These recurrences may follow a similar pattern, but more deep-seated catarrhal troubles may arise, possibly invading the sinuses (sinusitis), the lungs (bronchitis or other chest trouble) or the bladder (cystitis), each being treated, no doubt, with more suppressive drugs. Such a course of events will inevitably lead to the onset of chronic degenerative disease, of which rheumatic ailments are a most likely outcome.

Doctors and 'Spontaneous Remission'

A profoundly significant phenomenon may be observed, even in severe forms of disease and irrespective of the treatment, in that signs of recovery may appear. This is, of course, an indication that the natural healing power is asserting itself. The medical term for such an occurrence is 'spontaneous remission', but rarely if ever do doctors attempt to offer an explanation. There is an old saying, however, that 'Nature does the healing and the remedy gets the credit'. Nevertheless, where this happens, if the causes of the complaint remain unresolved further trouble must be expected in due course.

It should be understood that the progress from illness to better health is not necessarily uneventful. The intrinsic healing effort may give rise to certain reactions which, if they are not understood, may be misinterpreted. There may be signs for a while of inflammation, and possibly a rise in temperature, these symptoms being a manifestation of the body's efforts to achieve a process of tissue cleansing and elimination.

Medical theorists have admitted that the familiar reactions of fever (rise in body temperature) and inflammation have a 'benevolent intention' but these reactions are considered to be good only when they succeed. This is somewhat like saying that fire brigades are a good thing only if they put out every fire before it can cause any serious damage. However, it is not difficult to appreciate that when the body's resistance is lowered and the vital tissues are overburdened with toxic debris these natural reactions of fever and inflammation may only partially succeed in their efforts to restore health and to heal damaged tissues, in which event the end-result will be some further encroachment of degenerative disease. Natural treatment, if adopted and perseveringly followed, will remove any obstacles to healing and enable the natural efforts of the body to restore the highest possible level of health. This is the valid alternative to modern orthodox medicine.

Seeking the Alternative

There are now increasing numbers of persons who are seeking an alternative to chemotherapy and other medical methods, and I am convinced that many thousands more will welcome information and guidance as to how they may deal safely and effectively with the aches and pains which accompany rheumatism and arthritis and other forms of disease while building a better state of health and natural resistance.

The primary purpose of this book is to provide the necessary guidance and understanding which will enable such people to dispel as completely as possible the distressing and potentially crippling conditions which are characteristic of rheumatic ailments. For the great majority of sufferers this will serve to enrich the quality of life and increase the capacity for healthy activity, for the young (there are increasing numbers of rheumatic children), for the not-so-young, and also for those in the later years of life.

Those who wish to help themselves to such benefits, having completed the First Stage of nutritional therapy, may pass on immediately to the Second Stage.

The Nutritional Plan   Stage 2

On Rising: One tumbler of half-and-half pure unsweetened sub-acid fruit juice and vegetable juice prepared as in Stage 1. Fruit juices may be selected from the same choice and the vegetable juices may be varied, alternating carrot juice with raw beetroot juice or swede juice. Raw beetroot juice is very effective in helping to regulate the bowel while swede juice is a good source of vitamin C. Alternatively, a mixture of pure vegetable juices is sold by health food stores under the name *V8*. In this Second Stage it is desirable to vary the content of each of the meals, thus providing variety and interest while preserving the fundamental plan of nutrition. There are certain other advantages as will be explained later.

Breakfast: Alternate the following choices:
1   A serving of muesli (sometimes called Swiss breakfast), about three tablespoons with one tablespoon of bran. Moisten with milk (or a plant milk such as Plamil).
2   Ripe, raw fruit selected from the list in Stage 1, *or* a serving of dried fruit such as prunes or apricots or raisins gently stewed. (The skins of all fruits, including dried fruits, should be washed before they are

105

eaten.) Add 1–1½ tablespoons of wheatgerm. No beverage should be taken with breakfast.

Mid-morning: half a teaspoon each of Barmene or Tastex and Vecon or a similar yeast and vegetable extract stirred into a tumbler of hot water, taken hot or cold as desired. The drink may be made weaker or slightly stronger according to taste.

First Main Meal: A raw salad, as in Stage 1, selecting root and leafy ingredients as available. The grated root vegetables are particularly valuable in winter salads. For protein, have about 2 oz of cheese, either English Cheddar or a white cheese such as Wensleydale or Caerphilly, or cottage cheese, or a hard-boiled egg (free-range). All grated ingredients should be mixed at once with a dressing of yogurt or vegetable oil and lemon juice. This helps to avoid losses by oxidation of vitamin C and other nutrients. Include two slices of Ryvita or a similar wholegrain crispbread with the salad, or alternatively two slices of 100 per cent wholemeal stone-ground bread with a little butter or soft margarine.

To follow: Fresh raw ripe fruit (not citrus fruit) or fruit salad or yogurt (⅓–½ pint). The yogurt may be flavoured with a little honey or molasses.

Mid-afternoon: A small tumbler of pure unsweetened fruit juice, or a cup of weak tea without sugar or artificial sweetening.

Second Main Meal: A generous serving of one conservatively cooked green vegetable, with a smaller portion of one conservatively cooked root vegetable, such as carrot or onion, or a jacket potato (baked or boiled in its skin and eaten whole) with a little butter or soft margarine. For protein in this meal choose from a lightly poached egg with the green vegetable, or about 1½–2 oz of grated cheese, or 6–8 walnuts, or a portion of a texturised vegetable protein such as Protoveg (obtainable from health food stores).

To follow: A baked apple stuffed with raisins or one of the second courses detailed for the first main meal, but do not repeat one already served earlier in the day.

Later Evening: A small tumbler of unsweetened apple or grape juice or the vegetable beverage as for mid-morning.

The first and second main meals may be interchanged as may be convenient.

This *Second Stage* should be followed strictly for two or even three weeks.

In the conservative cooking of vegetables the following rules should be observed. Use a minimum of water (one or two cups according to the size of saucepan and the amount of vegetables). Bring the water to the boil and add the vegetables, cut or shredded. No salt or soda should be used. Place the lid on firmly and shake frequently to avoid burning. Cooking-time should not be more than 10–20 minutes with young vegetables. Older ones may take a little longer.

Avoid the use of aluminium saucepans; preferably use stainless steel or a good-quality enamel saucepan.

In preparing vegetables for cooking, root vegetables should not be peeled or scraped, but should be cleaned using a vegetable brush. Any blemishes should be cut out, of course. In the case of potatoes, if they are peeled before cooking they lose food value and may be fattening, whereas the jacket potato, eaten whole, appears to be non-fattening. This statement has been confirmed by the Potato Marketing Board.

It should be noted that, as in the First Stage, the sub-acid fruits are favoured in preference to the citrus fruits, particularly as regards oranges and orange juice, to which many rheumatic sufferers may react adversely. If citrus fruits and juices are introduced at a later date the emphasis should still be on the sub-acid fruits. Also, salt at table should be omitted or at least drastically reduced (see p. 166).

Rhubarb, with its high content of oxalic acid, should be avoided. Oxalates are commonly found in gallstones, kidneys stones and other similar deposits.

Reduction of Pain

Many rheumatic sufferers who have been taking anti-rheumatic, analgesic (pain-killer) drugs, perhaps with other symptom-suppressive drugs, soon find after closely following the recommended dietary treatment that they are able, with little or no difficulty, to reduce the dosage and in a majority of cases are able to dispense with drugs quite soon, provided that they persevere with the treatment in conjunction with other measures to be described in the following chapters. Not only will they experience true relief from their rheumatic symptoms but they will also benefit in being relieved of the *iatrogenic* diseases (side effects which are associated with all such drugs, both as short-term and long-term effects).

107

After completing Stages One and Two the whole programme should be repeated, starting with the two days semi-fast on fruit as before.

The restriction of fluids in the First and Second Stages is important, having proved most effective in cases of rheumatoid arthritis as well in other rheumatic conditions. It is also advisable to avoid drinking with meals, taking the beverages only between meals. If thirst is experienced it will most likely be due to a dry mouth or throat, caused by 'lazy' salivary glands or to a low-grade chronic throat inflammation, in which case it is usually sufficient to rinse the mouth and throat with a little water or diluted lemon juice.

Remember that most foods, particularly the fresh fruits and vegetables, have a large water content, and that this usually is water in its best and safest form.

Our choice of foods and the balance of our dietary are of paramount importance to our health. This, however, is certainly not the whole story of modern man's failure to adapt to so many of the factors introduced by the industrial society. Thus, there are a number of ways in which appropriate action may be taken towards restoring the balance of health and greatly reducing the incidence of the prevalent diseases, as indicated in the following chapters.

CHAPTER 16

Stages 4 and 5: Relief of Stress, Chemical and Mechanical

Further treatment is presented in detail and a balanced dietary of whole natural foods is prescribed.

The effectiveness of natural methods of pain relief is indicated, and the reduction of the possible effects of environmental pollution is discussed, including the practicalities of growing food organically.

A number of food facts and fallacies are discussed and the 'healing crisis' is explained.

The Nutritional Plan   Stage 4

Having completed Stage 3 – a repeat of the Second Stage of the nutritional plan – a further, but shortened, repetition of the same programme should be commenced immediately, consisting of a modified fast on pure vegetable and fruit juices (selected and prepared as directed on pp. 95–6), a small tumblerful being taken at intervals of from two to three hours. This semi-fast should be maintained for two or three days but no longer and it should be terminated with a day on fresh, raw fruit, the week being completed with four days on fruit and salad as in the First Stage (p. 96). Other good vegetable juices may be prepared in the same way as carrot juice (see pp. 95–6).

The Nutritional Plan   Stage 5

So far, treatment has almost invariably served to reduce pain and tension and thus should make it possible to reduce, and in many cases discontinue, the use of drugs. In addition, the use of simple measures of hydrotherapy, including cold-water compresses applied to inflamed and swollen joints, will help greatly to reduce pain (see pp. 163–5).

Many people imagine that dietary rules mean monotony and lack of variety and interest. In fact, even in Stages 1 and 2, the alternatives given provide for some degree of variety. Certainly, a balanced whole-food dietary should be accepted as a way of life if improvement in health is to continue and increase. To meet this need, guidance in planning the subsequent dietary and providing interest and variety may be obtained from *Everywoman's Wholefood Cook Book* by Vivien and Clifford Quick obtainable from health food stores and leading bookshops.

While continuing with the balanced dietary, the short fast on fruit and vegetable juices should be repeated regularly at intervals of from four to six weeks. During these fasting periods it is desirable to rest and relax as much as possible. When it is not possible to suspend working activities the short fruit fast may be substituted.

Symbiosis Disturbed

The programme of nutritional therapy as given is a lacto-vegetarian regimen. The flesh foods – meat, fish, poultry, etc. – are far from beneficial to rheumatic sufferers, having a strong tendency to create a relative acidosis, producing uric acid and other acidic and possibly toxic deposits. A further hazard associated with the flesh foods may arise from disturbance of the normal intestinal flora. This is the term for the many millions of bacteria which quite normally inhabit the intestine and which exist in a benevolent condition of *symbiosis* (see p.14). Their function is to inhibit the growth of harmful bacteria, assist the processes of digestion and manufacture a number of necessary vitamins.

Meat, fish and poultry and their various products are liable to disturb these benevolent micro-organisms, so much so that it has been stated reliably that over 80 per cent of food poisoning is due to the consumption of flesh foods. The occurrence of such disturbances appears to have been increased by the widespread use of antibiotic drugs, both as prescribed by doctors and in animal husbandry by veterinary surgeons; these drugs are also incorporated, in addition to steroids, in animal feeding-stuffs. The greatest danger may arise as a result of the development of strains of bacteria which have acquired resistance to antibiotics and thus are difficult to control.*

With many milder cases of gastro-intestinal trouble the cause is the same. The sufferer's doctor may make a somewhat ridiculous remark about having 'caught the bug which is going round' and possibly may prescribe more antibiotics. In such instances the wisest and usually most effective remedy is to take no food other than live natural yogurt, which helps to restore the normal healthy intestinal flora.

*The *acidophilons* culture of yogurt may assist in restoring normal intestinal flora.

In our present-day situation, food is by no means the only substance that we are likely to absorb from the polluted environment. As mentioned in Chapter 12, the enormous and rapid development of chemical technology over a few decades of this century, involving multimillion-pound industries, has been referred to as the 'chemical explosion'. Vast amounts of chemicals are being poured out, many of which are entirely strange to our terrestrial environment. Besides being highly poisonous, these substances affect almost every aspect of our life, being used in processing food, in agriculture, and in a thousand and one industries. Most of them have been developed from motives of profit and convenience, with insufficient knowledge of short-term effects and even less understanding of long-term effects, which are still in many cases problematical.

By one route or another, many of these substances find their way into our bodies to enter our bloodstream and tissues. Not least of these substances are the products of chemotherapy, the vast torrent of drugs almost all of which have side-effects which may cause drug-induced (iatrogenic) diseases. The statement of Sir Derrick Dunlop (see p. 60) has been confirmed by leading USA authorities. Dr Kelsey, of the Food and Drug Administration, has affirmed that 'the more potent and effective a drug is the more hazardous it usually is'. Again, Dr David P. Barr, addressing the American Medical Association in June 1955, pointed out that 'one of the great hazards in the use of potent drugs is their inherent toxicity'. He added that 'no agent that can modify the internal environment or organic integrity of the body can be used without hazard'.

Many of these chemicals, on entering our internal environment via the bloodstream and tissue fluid, may damage vital organs such as the liver and kidneys, in many cases irreparably. All such damaging influences play a large part in the ever-increasing incidence of chronic disease and premature senility.

This raises a question of great importance: what, if anything, can we do to defend ourselves from, or at least to minimise, such environmental hazards?

No doubt many doctors consider that warnings of drug dangers should be toned down because they may cause anxiety to patients, especially the long-term users such as chronic rheumatics and arthritics. Such suppression of facts might be excusable if in fact there were no valid alternative to offer the patient and, unfortunately, most doctors appear to have none to offer. *Meanwhile, there is a growing realisation of the need for an alternative to orthodox chemotherapy. This book is concerned solely with that alternative.*

Natural methods, based on the three main headings of disease

111

causation (see p. 67), are unique in that they do more than treat symptoms and are primarily concerned with the restoration and maintenance of positive health and the accompanying sense of well-being, with relief of painful symptoms, in which there may be little or no need for analgesic or anti-rheumatic drugs. In this way we may take steps to increase our natural resistance to many environmental hazards, a fact that environmental scientists are beginning to appreciate. Thus, Jack Lucas, in his book *Our Polluted Food,* mentions that 'the state of health enjoyed by the individual and the adequacy of the diet may also be factors in modifying and adapting to any toxic effects'. Other writers, including Dr Max Warmbrand of the USA, have made similar statements. Few of these writers – other than Dr Warmbrand – have made any positive suggestions as to how the desirable state of health is to be achieved and maintained.

Removing Toxic Encumbrance

Following the specific plan in Stage 1 for the removal of toxic encumbrance, the main function of the balanced, whole-food plan is that it provides the essential way to rebuild positive health, freeing joints and muscles and constantly improving the quality and tensile strength of body tissues. This will result in progressive easing of discomfort and pain and thus will greatly facilitate the discontinuance of drug taking with a minimum of withdrawal symptoms. This applies even with steroid drugs, although in some cases the withdrawal may best be accomplished in two or more stages.

Further easing of pain may result from the restriction of fluids and the reduction of salt and sugar. It is also helpful to omit strong condiments. Barmene or Tastex may be used as a condiment or flavouring, but it should be used in moderation, as in the case of mustard, for example.

Another very helpful procedure for easing painful and/or inflamed joints is hydrotherapy, using cold-water compresses (see pp. 120, 163).

The other major causes of pollution are the modern practices of using chemicals in agriculture and animal husbandry and in food processing.

Since the publication of Rachel Carson's book, *Silent Spring,* in 1962, there has been growing realisation of the dangers of using chemicals in farming and gardening, and consequently there is increased interest in produce grown organically without the use of chemical fertilisers, poison sprays and insecticides. There is a much-reduced tendency to refer to those who grow food by natural means, with the use of compost, as 'the muck and mystery people'.

Organically Grown Food

Many readers will be able and keen to grow some produce by these natural methods, even though this may entail digging up part of the lawn. Even those who have only a paved yard or patio may be surprised at the amount of good natural food that may be grown by the 'container gardening' methods.

In addition to the health benefits to be derived from such wholesome food, there are other advantages, such as enjoyment of the delicious tastes and textures of fresh, unadulterated fruits and vegetables and also the satisfaction of saving money in comparison with the costs of relatively inferior commercial products.

Fortunately, there are now increasing numbers of farms and market gardens producing organically grown food, and information concerning them may be obtained from organisations listed in the Epilogue (pp. 219–20). Readers may also contact their local health food stores, who may know organic growers in their vicinity. In this respect, health food stores are also performing a valuable complementary service in that they aim to market many foods which carry the assurance that they are organically produced and as free as possible from the thousands of chemicals used in modern food processing. Also, they have pioneered the introduction of vegetable protein preparations which meet the requirements of palatability and texture and so are rapidly gaining popularity while being free from the many disadvantages and dangers of flesh foods – meat, fish, poultry, etc.

What about Vitamins and Minerals?

Many people are very reluctant to accept the need for alterations in their way of life. They may ask how claims concerning the supremacy of the *whole-food balanced plan of nutrition* are justified. Any readers who are looking for an easy way to health and who wish to cling to old habits of dietary may hopefully imagine that a faulty diet may be made good by taking liberal amounts of vitamin and mineral supplements.

Such a course of fragmentation is likely to lead to disappointing results, very different from the indisputable benefits obtained by adopting a whole-food diet plan.

The ideal source of the many essential vitamins, minerals, enzymes, trace elements and other factors, known and unknown, is and always will be in their natural form and context, through a balanced diet of whole natural foods.

When for any reason the dietary has been seriously deficient for a considerable time it may be desirable to take supplements in suitable amounts as supportive therapy in order to make good such

113

deficiencies. This may apply under certain circumstances where for domestic, occupational or other reasons a well balanced diet is not immediately practicable.

It should also be understood that very high doses of certain vitamins and mineral supplements may possibly do more harm than good, and we sometimes find them listed with the medical information concerning the side-effects of drugs.

The mechanical engineer will realise the essential interdependence and quality requirements of every component, small or large, of a complex machine. Similarly, we who are in charge of our own vastly more complex vital organism – the human body – should have some knowledge of it needs. In earlier chapters examples have been given of the physical excellence and relative freedom from disease of many isolated communities who have lived for many centuries on their native whole foods. These examples are in sharp contrast with the physical conditions and nutritional diseases arising directly and indirectly from the widespread use of the over-processed and devitalised foods of modern civilisation.

Further confirmation comes from the observation that members of the same primitive races coming to live in modern civilised communities suffer after a comparatively short time from many of the diseases of our modern civilisation. Moreover, as might be expected, yet further confirmation comes from those who adopt a pure, whole-food balanced dietary which is regularly found to restore them to health.

In addition to the factor of wholeness and freedom from chemical pollution there is a further important consideration, namely the relative proportions and balance between the various classes of nutrients. Considerable guidance in this respect has been acquired by means of our present-day knowledge of nutritional science.

Further Food Facts

Readers who are not already familiar with the following facts may find these points interesting and instructive:

1 *Carbohydrates.* The carbohydrates are the starches and sugars, the concentrated and processed forms being bread, cakes, pastries, biscuits and various cereals and the sugars used as sweeteners and for the manufacture of sweets, confectionery and many more commodities, the total amounts consumed being greater than ever before in the history of mankind.

2 *Fats.* The fats are found in solid form as meat, butter, lard, etc., and

the oils (which are fats with a low melting-point) are found as fish oils and as vegetable oils in nuts, grains and seeds, etc. (for example corn or maize, sunflower seeds, peanuts and olives).

The carbohydrates and fats are principally concerned with providing energy (expressed as calories), but the fats also provide a source of the fat-soluble vitamins.

An excess of either carbohydrates or fats, far from providing us with abundant energy, is more likely to produce excess weight and result in a condition of obesity (see pp. 90–2), which is largely responsible for so many forms of degenerative disease. Also, among the carbo-hydrates the 'rogue foods' predominate in the form of refined cereals, white flour, polished rice and white sugar (see pp. 169–70).

3   *Proteins.* The normal function of the protein foods is to ensure the growth, development, replacement and repair of all body tissues. The basic materials of all body structures and organs are composed of proteins, nature's building blocks. The main sources of protein are the flesh foods (meat, fish, poultry, etc.), the dairy products (milk, cheese, eggs, etc.), and the vegetable proteins such as nuts, peas, beans, lentils, etc. The calorific value of proteins is similar to that of the carbohydrates, but they should not be regarded basically as a source of energy.

Proteins are extremely complex substances and are present in all plant and animal tissues. The relatively simple units from which the proteins are constructed are known as *amino-acids,* of which about twenty different kinds have been identified.

Most proteins are constructed of about 15–18 individual amino-acids, and the complexity of their structure may be imagined from the fact that a single molecule of muscle protein contains about 3,500 molecules of amino-acids with a molecular weight of about 1 million. In this way, from the moment of conception the unique property of protein is responsible for growth, maintenance, repair and replacement of tissues for as long as we live.

Protein molecules are exactly replicated by means of a remarkable process mediated by complex substances present in the nucleus of the living cell. These are the nucleic acids known as DNA and RNA. In this fundamental process involving the nucleoproteins, the complex molecules are able to act as a pattern or template, attracting and linking amino-acids in the same sequence, thus forming a duplicate molecule which then splits off. By this process, a new protein molecule is produced, thus satisfying the body's needs for the building and repair of its tissues.

In this wonderful process RNA is important in the synthesis of protein, while DNA is said to control the genetic processes transmitting hereditary characteristics from generation to generation.

Thus it is that little Johnnie may have a Roman nose like grandpapa and other ancestors. He may also, of course, inherit less desirable traits in similar manner.

An equally important function of proteins in the living cell is the production of a number of protein substances termed *enzymes,* which are responsible for the regulation and control of specific biochemical reactions. Some enzymes are simple proteins and others are much more complex. Collectively, these natural chemicals act and interact to produce other enzymes and thus to regulate almost all living processes, so that the sum total of all these spontaneous activities constitutes the chemical mechanism of life itself.

It is a sobering thought that in every one of the thousands of millions of living cells in the human body there are hundreds of chemical reactions taking place simultaneously, each one being specifically under enzyme control. Moreover, the study of these enormously complex intercellular reactions is limited by the fact that once the cell membrane is breached the whole system is disrupted. In brief, the living cell is, and is likely to remain, inscrutable.

These growth and repair processes, rather than energy production, are the true functions of protein. While it is important that a balanced diet shall include sufficient protein for its essential purposes, most civilised diets contain too much protein, and this excess may be a factor in the development of rheumatic conditions due to the production of toxic acid end-products, including uric acid, in addition, perhaps, to overloading the kidneys.

The High-protein Diet Fallacy

Many slimming plans are based on high-protein diets for the reason that protein in excess of normal requirements produces a reaction named *Specific Dynamic Action* which may cause the metabolic rate to rise by 20 per cent or even as much as 35 per cent, thus producing extra heat which tends to 'burn up' tissue. In other words, it may act in the manner of a wasting fever. This is certainly not a desirable way to reduce weight, and it may indeed be indirectly responsible for an increase in the incidence of rheumatism and arthritis; in this sense, protein 'is not for burning'.

In general, the inhabitants of the more highly civilised countries eat from two and a half to three times the necessary amount of protein. This was verified in 1909 by the American physiologist R. H. Chittenden, with lengthy experiments on volunteers, students and soldiers which demonstrated that moderate amounts of protein with dietary were adequate and the reduction was beneficial.

More recently, L. E. Holt, in America (1962), showed in animal feeding experiments that a similarly reduced protein intake resulted in higher resistance to stresses such as heavy exercise, injuries, infections, parasitic infestations and unfavourable environmental temperatures.

Again, at the 1974 Conference in Rome on the future of food supplies, it was reported that requirements for protein had been set far too high in the past. A further ancient fallacy has also been exposed, namely the idea that only animal proteins (meat, etc.) were to be considered as 'first-class protein'. It is now admitted that a dietary of mixed vegetable proteins which includes both grains and pulses is in no way second-class or nutritionally inferior.

In adopting the recommended, whole-food, balanced dietary, including dairy produce, there need be no question as to the quality and adequacy of its protein content, but it avoids the disadvantages of excess protein intake. Incidentally, while the emphasis is mainly on the concentrated forms of protein it should not be forgotten that a majority of all vegetable foods contain a small but significant proportion of protein, for example, wholemeal flour contains 8·9 per cent, and there are smaller amounts in many vegetables, including the potato. The pulses, particularly the soya bean and other beans, peas, lentils, etc., are rich sources of excellent quality protein.

4   Fruits and Vegetables

The fourth and last group of nutrients is in many respects the most important. There are the fruits and vegetables. All natural whole foods contain some vitamins and minerals, but the fresh raw fruits and vegetables are rich and valuable sources of these essential food factors, including the necessary trace minerals.

Conventional dietaries invariably contain a preponderance of carbohydrates, fats and proteins and relatively few fresh raw fruits and vegetables. The latter may be still further depleted by cooking, with a resultant loss of minerals and vitamins, especially vitamin C. Such losses may be minimised by cooking conservatively (see pp. 106–7), but to avoid such serious losses it is imperative that at least 50 per cent of fruits and vegetables are eaten as fresh as possible in the form of raw salads and ripe raw fruits. The foods in groups 1, 2 and 3 – the carbohydrates, proteins and fats are all acid-forming, whereas the fruits and vegetables are alkaline in reaction. With the preponderance of acid-forming foods in the conventional dietary the homoeostatic acid/alkali balance to maintain a pH in the region of 7·4 is constantly under stress (see pp. 39–40 and 96). If this danger is to be avoided, the dietary balance should be adjusted to provide approximately the following proportions of the major nutrients:

Carbohydrates	20 per cent
Proteins	15 per cent
Fats	5 per cent
Fruits and vegetables	60 per cent

The balanced, whole-food dietary plan fulfils these proportionate requirements.

It should be observed that the acids that are normally in fruits do *not* cause acidity, since they are neutralised in digestion, leaving a residue of alkaline salts.

Some readers may at first experience some degree of digestive disturbance, perhaps with flatulence, in following the dietary plan. This should be only a temporary condition while the system adjusts itself to the necessary change in diet. It may be helped by having only sub-acid fruits for a time, while salads and raw vegetables should be easily digested if shredded finely and immediately dressed with natural yogurt. It should be noted that when cucumber is peeled it is usually indigestible, but if it is eaten with the skin it is usually easily digested.

The proportions of the various food factors in the balanced dietary do not place the emphasis on the so-called calorie foods, for while the 'energy foods' – the carbohydrates and fats – are essential, to increase them beyond the recommended proportions may do more harm than good, especially in their refined forms (white sugar, white flour, etc.). Fortunately, the slogan 'sugar for energy' seems to have disappeared.

The developments of nutritional science in recent years, and much practical experience, have confirmed the foregoing recommendations. Alone among orthodox nutritionists, A. Barbara Callow, Reader in Nutrition at Oxford, was decades in advance of her colleagues when she wrote in the early 1950s: 'To most people, energy means vitality and vigour, and it must be admitted that energy of this kind is concerned far more with such food factors as mineral elements and vitamins than with the calorie value of our food.'

These most precious vitamins and minerals are present in their natural holistic forms (see p. 88) in the whole-food plan here presented. Incidentally, since the 1950s a number of additional vitamins and minerals, including trace elements, have been identified in natural foods. These and doubtless still more yet to be discovered have been present in the traditional foods of mankind from his earliest days before the dawn of history until now, when intensive food processing threatens to upset the balance of nature and with it the balance of health.

Sugar, which was virtually unknown to our ancestors before the seventeenth century, is now being consumed in vastly greater amounts than ever before. Certainly, the less refined sugars are distinctly less harmful than refined white sugar, but it is advisable to reduce the intake of *all* sugar. A little honey may be used, but it should be remembered that this too is a very concentrated food. The use of artificial sweeteners is also undesirable, since the safety of their long-term use is suspect. It is far better to accept the need for a reduction of sugar, and you may be surprised how soon the craving for sweet things may decline. We need not be slaves to our tastes and habits. It is not so difficult to exchange an old bad taste or habit for a new and better one, and the desire to revert will eventually vanish.

The Healing Crisis

Another important matter has to be explained and understood. Common sense should enable us to understand that just as there is a time factor in all vital processes, and particularly in the processes of healing, it should not be expected that progress will be uniform and uneventful. At some point in the curative process, what has been termed a 'healing crisis' is likely to develop. This is in accordance with the fact that most disease symptoms represent the spontaneous curative effort of the vital system of the body. A healing crisis may take the form of an acute reaction such as a cold, with copious mucus discharge, perhaps with a rise in temperature, aching of limbs and joints, and possibly a skin rash probably of the type known as a 'rheumatic rash' or a 'drug rash'. These are all signs that the body is engaged in the task of getting rid of debris which, while in the tissues, may have been a direct cause of the rheumatic condition.

The term 'crisis' means a decisive moment or turning-point, and this is to be recognised as being a healing effort which, if treated, rightly, will be followed by a proportionate improvement in the arthritis or other form of rheumatism, and should subsequently result in a substantial improvement in general health and vitality, provided that the healing crisis is treated rightly. This means that, first, no drugs should be given – no antibiotics and not even the familiar medicines such as aspirin, paracetamol, etc.

This natural process should be assisted by fasting, taking only moderate amounts of water or pure fruit and vegetable juices at intervals of from two to three hours.

At this stage, probably, well-meaning friends or relations may try to insist on 'taking something to get the temperature down', etc. Be sure

119

to remember that the rise in temperature is a *curative reaction* and that the temperature (fever) will normalise itself when its beneficial work is done. The feverish phase may be further aided by means of tepid sponging of the limbs and trunk. Another helpful procedure is the use of cold-water compresses as follows.

Wring out some cotton or linen sheeting of suitable size to wrap round the trunk – from the armpits to the waist – when folded in two or three layers. This cold wet compress (well wrung out and *not* dripping) is then covered with dry woollen material such as flannel or a small blanket. A smaller compress may be applied to the neck. Within about ten minutes the initial cold feeling should be succeeded by a warm reaction generated by the body heat, and thereafter it should remain warm. If a feeling of coldness persists it may be that the sheeting was not wrung out sufficiently. If the warm reaction is poor as may happen with elderly persons and in cases of low vitality, hot-water bottles may be applied to the feet and each side of the body.

These compresses are most helpful in reducing pain, swelling and inflammation in joints, etc. Such a pack may be put on at night and removed in the morning, by which time it should be dry. In a fever, the compresses may be put on several times during the day, sponging the trunk with tepid water before applying a fresh compress. Usually the temperature should return to normal within two or three days.

Fasting in Fever

The fast should be broken by taking sub-acid fruit, and the balanced whole-food dietary should then be resumed.

Managed in this way, a healing crisis should not only result in improvement of the rheumatic condition but should also ensure that any similar crisis – should one occur – is likely to be milder and should be treated in the same way. While recognising the importance of nutrition and other environmental factors in determining health and disease, the influence of body mechanics must never be underrated. Moreover, neither body mechanics nor body chemistry should be considered in isolation, for these ruling factors in our existence are interdependent to an extent which generally is not sufficiently appreciated.

Life is movement; when the pulsation of the heart and blood-vessels ceases the end of life is imminent. The energy needed by the body machine is constantly supplied by its biochemical reactions, while the energy expended by the body machine mainly determines its biochemical integrity. The nutrient factors in food are not available to the internal environment until they have passed through the alimentary tract and have been adapted by the digestive juices so as to be assimilated into the bloodstream. This is a mechanical process, as well as a biochemical one. First, there is the process of mastication, in which the first stage of digestion is effected by the jaws and tongue acting with the saliva – which is the first of the digestive juices, and which contains the enzyme *ptyalin* – to begin the process of starch digestion. Failure to masticate thoroughly impairs the first stage of digestion.

The Painful Jaw

Quite commonly, two factors may interfere with mastication, namely decayed teeth (or ill fitting dentures) and arthritis in the jaw-joints. If ill fitting dentures or painful teeth prevent thorough mastication, do not delay seeing your dentist. As a temporary measure, instead of existing on pappy foods (possibly washed down with tea or other fluid), it is better to mince or finely grate raw salads and other natural foods and mix each mouthful thoroughly with the saliva before swallowing. If jaw-joints are affected with arthritis then, in addition to the dietary (Stages 1 and 2), they may be treated with alternating hot- and cold-water compresses (see *hydrotherapy*, pp. 163–5) and exercised daily with gentle movements, so as to restore full movement. There are three types of movement of the lower jaw, straight open and close, forward and backward, and side to side. Practise while observing the jaw movements in a mirror.

Following mastication and swallowing, the food is mixed and propelled through the stomach and intestine by vigorous wave-like movements known as peristalsis, so as to be exposed to the gastric and intestinal digestive juices until the liquefied nutrients produced by these mechanical and biochemical activities are ready to be absorbed through the walls of the intestine into the bloodstream.

These vital processes – the glandular secretions and the spontaneous movements of the muscles situated in the inner linings of the alimentary tract are largely under the control of a part of the autonomic nervous system over which we have no direct conscious control. Thus they may be affected by numerous biochemical and mechanical influences, and partly by nervous tension and other emotional states which may give rise to health disturbances in various ways. Such subconscious disturbances are termed *psychosomatic* (literally 'mind-body') influences, and they will be considered under the third group of the three principal factors of disease causation.

But first, the incidence of body mechanics as they concern the problems of rheumatism and arthritis must be more fully considered.

121

CHAPTER 17

How the Body Works

This chapter explains practical procedures and remedial exercises for restoring movement and reducing the impairment of joints, muscles and other vital structures. Techniques are discussed which help to release nervous tension and correct shallow breathing and faulty posture.

Few people give conscious thought to the mechanical processes of our daily life. Even in learning the skills to play a musical instrument or an athletic game or some other form of physical skill, much thought and expertise may be devoted to acquiring the specific skill but often insufficient attention is given to the use of the body-machine with maximum ease and efficiency. This may be described as 'end-gaining', with concentration only on the objective without due attention being given to what is being done in the process, possibly incurring unnecessary occupational stresses which, if habitual, may give rise to excessive wear and tear.

Apart from the attrition caused by such misuse of the self, the latter is a principal cause of accident proneness. These persons will suffer sooner or later from unnecessary fatigue, muscles will weaken and the natural protective reflexes will be impaired, so that in addition to the constant occupational stresses there may be the effects of accidental injury which should have been avoidable.

Factors of Mechanical Stress

Remembering that there are many causes of rheumatism and arthritis, sufferers from these complaints should realise that mechanical stress factors must be included among the causes of these complaints and therefore steps should be taken to remedy any such inefficient habits, the effects of which may be more far-reaching than is generally realised. Also, others in whom rheumatic conditions are not yet apparent will be well advised to assess the efficiency of their body mechanics and to take action to correct such errors without delay.

This also may prove to be an important form of preventive medicine. The most prevalent of these habitual errors are the following:

1 Overeagerness and haste to reach a particular goal.
2 Negative emotions of fear, frustration, etc.
3 Misguidance from parents, teachers and others which, however well intended, may have been quite incorrect. All these factors may be the cause of *nervous tension*.

Those who suffer from nervous tension realise this to some extent and may say that they have tried to relax but have not succeeded. Their failure is attributable mainly to the fact that the mechanism of nervous tension is not well understood, and so a brief explanation is necessary.

All mobile parts of the human skeleton have joints which allow for necessary movements, most of which are under our conscious control.

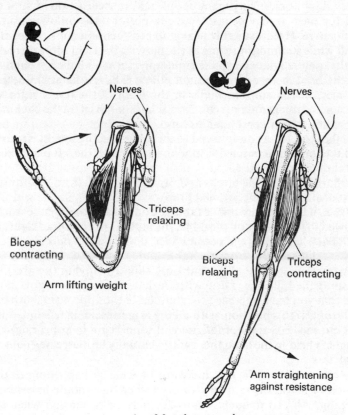

Nerves

Triceps
relaxing

Biceps
contracting

Arm lifting weight

Nerves

Biceps
relaxing

Triceps
contracting

Arm straightening
against resistance

6   Muscles at work

The joint-to-joint attachment is effected by means of ligaments and muscles. The former are tough, fibrous and flexible, but not elastic; the

123

popular term 'gristle' is more familiar to most people. Normally, ligaments are sufficently slack to allow full movement while preventing dislocation of the joint.

The mechanism of bones and joints involves a system of levers which are operated by muscles. Each muscle is effectively a small engine which is capable of one movement only. It contracts when it is triggered by a nervous impulse and when the contraction ceases the muscle becomes relaxed and inactive. In its one simple act of contraction the muscle shortens, thickens and hardens, thus moving the bones and joints which it serves.

Figure 6 illustrates one of the movements most familiar to us – the bending of the arm at the elbow by the contraction of the biceps and brachialis muscles. Very many people take muscle action for granted, and for them it may be instructive to perform the following simple manoeuvre. Hold a suitably heavy object, such as a book, in the right hand while standing or sitting at a table with the right forearm resting on the table. Lightly grasp the right upper arm with the left hand and lift the book by bending the right elbow. The left hand will feel the muscles, biceps and brachialis in the front of the upper right arm harden and thicken as they contract, while the muscle at the back of the upper arm (the triceps) remains limp.

If the forearm is now lowered to the table, and the weight is released and the forearm is pressed firmly on to the table, the left hand should feel the triceps muscle situated at the back of the upper arm contract and harden, while the biceps and brachialis in the front of the upper right arm will become soft and limp.

Then, if the pressure on the table is stopped and the right forearm is allowed to rest limply on the table, the muscles of the upper right arm, both back and front, will become soft, limp and less bulky.

Next, lift the arm from the table and poise the clenched fist as if preparing to strike a blow (but only slightly moving the arm). On grasping the right upper arm with the left hand as before you should find that you have tightened the muscles of the upper arm, both back and front. If this position, with all the arm muscles in tension, is held without moving, signs of fatigue will soon begin to appear, and if a weight is held in the hand there will eventually be increasing pain and weakness.

Most people are largely unaware of what is happening in their muscles when at work, at play, or even when they should be resting or sleeping. All too frequently muscles may be in tension when they should be relaxed and at rest. This may affect your health adversely in a number of ways. The simple tests just described should have demonstrated and made you consciously aware of the following facts:

1 The normal behaviour of a muscle at work, i.e. when contracting.
2 That by its simple mechanism of contraction a muscle will produce movement of its associated joint in one direction, but that
reversal of the movement is effected by another muscle. Each
of these muscles is said to be the *opponent* of the other. Thus,
normally, when one muscle is working its opponent should
relax so as not to resist the desired movement.
3 That it is possible for the two opponent muscles to be working at
the same time in opposite directions, thus hindering or inhibiting
any movement. When this occurs the signs of fatigue are apt to
appear sooner than they would when the muscles are engaged
in normal unopposed movement.

Nervous Tension Reduces Efficiency

Muscles are, in fact, highly efficient biological engines. Whereas a
steam engine puts out between 7 and 20 per cent of its energy in work,
muscles expend from 25 to 30 per cent of their energy in mechanical
work, when functioning normally. *Nervous tension* is one of the
principal causes of reduced muscular efficiency. Not only does it
interfere with the co-ordination of movement, but it also almost
invariably means that muscle contraction persists even in the absence
of useful and intentional movement. The tightened jaw, the clenched
fist, even the tense facial muscles, which are termed 'the muscles
of expression', all may convey the impression of negative emotions such as fear, anger, anxiety etc., or conversely of joy, love or
serenity.

It might be imagined that merely to recognise the existence of
emotional causes of nervous tension would suffice to release the
useless and potentially harmful associated muscular tensions.
Unfortunately, it frequently does not prove to be so simple and
spontaneous. Lengthy psychiatric treatments may fail to help, and
these have now been replaced largely by the use of mood-influencing
drugs (tranquillisers, muscle relaxants and anti-depressant drugs),
many of which are among the most poisonous and harmful drugs now
in use. Never can it be said that they achieve a satisfactory solution of
the problems of nervous tension.

On the other hand there is a substantially different approach which
is frequently highly successful: instead of the mind-body (psychosomatic) approach, a form of body-mind (somatico-psychic)
technique may be used. The latter has proved to be extremely helpful,
with few exceptions, even in many patients who have been regarded as
'difficult cases'.

125

Self-awareness

If you have applied to yourself the three simple tests of muscle action, a further procedure to increase self-awareness and conscious management of muscles and groups of muscles should be practised as follows. Lie on your back on a bed or divan or some other comfortable surface, making yourself as limp as possible. Proceed to tighten muscles in sequence from your head to your toes. First, tighten your face muscles, as in a frown and hold tight for a count or eight. Now, if you let go and convert the frown to a peaceful smile, accompanied by a feeling of relief, you may find that you have spontaneously exhaled an easy, pleasant breath of the type known as a 'sigh of relief'. Next, close the eyes and squeeze hard. Hold for a count of eight then release the tension in the eyelids with another 'sigh of relief'. Repeat the same procedure with the jaws, clenching the teeth tightly while your fingertips are placed over the jaw-joints just in front of the lobes of the ears. Your fingers should feel the muscles which close the jaws tighten strongly. Again, release the jaw tension with a sigh of relief.

Repeat this tighten-and-let-go procedure with the hands, then the forearms, the upper arms and the shoulders – raise the latter strongly in a shrugging movement and then pause and drop them. Continue with the shoulder-blades, pulling them together and releasing them, then the buttocks, the thighs, the calves and finally the toes. You should conclude with the sigh-of-relief 'letting go' breath in each case. Throughout this routine be sure to study these processes and your accompanying sensations, particularly appreciating the sense of relief each time you release a tight muscle-group.

Having repeated this routine a number of times, it should be possible to distinguish clearly between states of tension and states of relaxation, and furthermore to discover hitherto unrealised habits of tension and so be able to discard these habits to great advantage. Where rheumatic tissues become increasingly painful on tightening the muscles, the tension should naturally be modified accordingly.

Careful note should be taken of the sense of relief resulting from the release of tension in the muscle groups. The benefits which accrue from the ability to relax are not confined to the purely physical effects. The physical release, by contributing to the generally enhanced sense of well-being which results from the nutritional treatments already described, tends to achieve considerable and often complete discharge of the negative emotional states which are associated with nervous tension, thus revealing the hitherto not understood processes by which such undesirable psychosomatic states become established.

In describing the muscle-tension testing exercises, the most important of all muscle groups has not been included for the reason that it requires special consideration and treatment, namely the *muscles of breathing.*

The Way to Better Breathing

The principal muscle of breathing is the *diaphragm,* the dome-shaped muscular organ which separates the chest from the abdomen. The working of the diaphragm is assisted and partially controlled by the *intercostal muscles,* which are situated between each pair of ribs. These muscles are under dual control, both voluntary and automatic. The lifelong continuance of breathing while we are awake or asleep is automatically assured and is speeded or retarded according to the degree of physical activity. Also, the range of movement of the chest, deep or shallow, is similarly regulated. For these all-important needs the breathing mechanism is served and controlled by a special respiratory centre situated in the brain.

Of comparable importance is the conscious, voluntary ability to control both the movement and the force of breathing. We can hold the breath for a short time, we can increase its force by blowing, or control it in singing or playing a musical wind-instrument, and so forth.

Also, the breathing process is affected reflexly in a number of ways for our protection and well-being, such as when we cough to clear a lung obstruction, or sneeze to clear the nasal passages, or when breathing responds to our emotional states so that excitement causes the breath-rate to be increased along with the heart-beat. All these reflex responses are monitored and controlled through the autonomic nervous system. Also, the depth and rapidity of breathing are affected by the secretions of the endocrine glands. The automatic control of breathing prevents the onset of acidosis (lowering of pH, see pp. 39–40) by increasing the depth and rate of breathing as necessary to expel excess carbon dioxide, which is the body's principal gaseous waste.

Thus the mechanical functions of breathing are directly geared to disturbances of body chemistry and also to the psychosomatic reactions which arise from emotional disturbances. The spontaneous regulation of breathing provides a convincing example in support of the basic concept by which causes of disease are classified under three main headings (see p. 67).

Unfortunately, bad breathing is a common characteristic of civilised man. The most common error is referred to as 'shallow breathing'. Almost invariably it means that the range of respiratory movements is limited. Its effects may be far-reaching; living cells may be partially deprived of life-giving oxygen, while failing to eliminate efficiently the acidic waste, carbon dioxide, which when excessively retained may cause blueness in the lips, the eyes, the hands and feet, etc.

Shallow breathing may also reduce the circulatory efficiency of the body fluids, the blood and lymph. To emphasise its importance a brief explanation of this mechanism is needed.

The blood, after discharging its carbon dioxide in the lungs and recharging its oxygen supply, returns to the heart to be pumped forcibly by that organ, assisted by the elastic recoil of the arteries, to all parts of the body. (This force is what is known as the 'blood pressure', which obviously is highly necessary for the purpose it serves.) After passing through the network of very tiny blood-vessels (the capillaries) the absorbed blood, having given up its oxygen and absorbed carbon dioxide, passes into the veins in which the pressure is much lower. This venous blood has to be returned to the heart. It will be realised that in order to return the blood from the feet and legs to the heart in the standing posture a considerable gravitational force has to be overcome. This upward flow is, however, assisted by the squeezing effect of muscular movements, and in the case of the longer veins there are valves situated at intervals to prevent backward flow. When we are at rest, the circulatory movements of the blood and lymph is assisted by the constant movement of the *muscles of breathing*. Even while we sleep these muscles are always working to maintain the circulatory activities which affect every living cell and which must proceed continuously whether we are awake or asleep, standing or lying down, active or passive. Clearly, we need to correct faulty breathing, and especially 'shallow breathing'.

First, it is necessary to understand what is meant by 'shallow breathing' and what are the reasons for the faulty use of this most natural of all vital functions. Fortunately it is one over which we may exercise conscious control.

When we inhale, the total volume of the thorax (Figure 7) increases as the diaphragm descends and the ribs move outwards and upwards in a movement resembling that of a bucket handle.

The circulation of tissue fluid or lymph is not directly effected by the heart pump but is dependent on the movement of muscles and, in particular, the movements of the diaphragm in breathing. The outgoing breath is normally effected by an elastic recoil of the same muscles. We can, however, extend exhalation voluntarily to force a further expulsion of breath, a potential which is precisely controlled by trained singers and performers on wind instruments. The total change in chest volume during this process involves the movement of more than a hundred joints if we include those where the spinal vertebrae meet the ribs and where the ribs meet the breastbone (sternum).

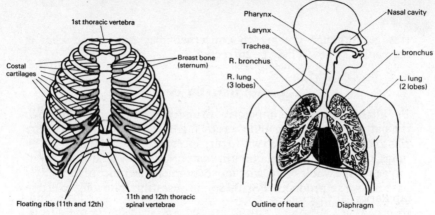

7(a) and (b)   The respiratory organs

It is not difficult to identify most of the ways in which the movements of breathing may become restricted, thus causing a reduction in the total breath excursion. First, patients who have suffered from chest troubles – such as pleurisy, rheumatic fever, influenza, etc. – may be left with a chronic condition in which there is a loss of mobility of the joints, or pleural adhesions, and/or rheumatic conditions in the joints of the ribs and spine, and fibrositis affecting the muscles of breathing. Stiffness of the joints and relative weakness of the muscles may also result from lack of exercise and this is one of the early signs of rheumatic disease.

Breath-holding is also a frequent faulty habit associated with nervous tension, often resulting from misguided advice at home and in school. Unfortunately the military idea of standing stiffly to attention (often responsible for the collapse of soldiers on parade), although now largely out of date, has led to instructions to children and others to 'hold your tummy in', 'tuck your tail in', 'pull your shoulders back', 'brace yourself for the effort', etc., all of which are the language of tension to the extent that the resulting fatigue may be both frustrating and exhausting. Unfortunately, similar misguided ideas have been promoted by some 'keep-fit' and 'health-and-beauty' systems and are likely to cause rather than correct faulty posture. Further inhibition of the natural movements of deep breathing may result from the use of restrictive clothing, tight belts, corsetry, etc., which restrict the free movement of the diaphragm, and abdomen and lower ribs.

Shallow breathing may also result solely or partly from what have been termed negative emotional states.

When, for one reason or another, the movements of the diaphragm and lower ribs are restricted, exaggerated efforts may be made to compensate by increasing the movements of the upper parts of the

129

ribcage, although the person concerned may not realise what is happening or how it may be corrected.

Loosen your stiff joints

For all these reasons it is imperative to undertake measures to improve the pattern of breathing and thereby increase the movements of the ribs and diaphragm, which will in turn increase the vital capacity of the lungs, thus ensuring the maximum ventilation and a greater supply of oxygen to the whole body, with more complete clearance of the body's gaseous waste products. For these purposes the following exercise should be practised daily.

Exercise No. 1 (see illustration below)

Lying on the back, with the hands on the upper abdomen, exhale forcibly as completely as possible (imagine you are blowing a long note on a bugle). Then, while holding the breath, draw in the abdominal muscles strongly and hold the contraction for about two seconds. Proceed to take in a long, slow breath so that the movement commences with expansion in the abdominal region and continues with expansion of the lower ribcage, and then the upper ribs. At full expansion, give three or four vigorous sniffs so as to widen the chest still further. Exhale, letting the breath go rapidly so as to become completely relaxed, then continue to breathe quietly. With the hands still on the abdomen, the relaxed abdominal muscles should be felt to be quietly rising and falling rhythmically. Repeat the complete exercise up to five or six times. Lastly, take an easy full breath and at once let it go.

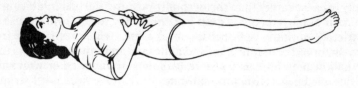

This should be the type of breath referred to as the 'sigh of relief'. When properly carried out, this complete exercise should establish a natural, easy rhythm of breathing deep, unhurried and relaxed, relieving any previous tendency to breathlessness.

Most, if not all, sufferers from rheumatic ailments are subject to a greater or lesser degree of nervous tension and shallow breathing. To them the benefits resulting from the expansion of breath capacity, with increased mobility of joints, may prove to be a major factor in their recovery.

In addition to the improved ventilation of the lungs, a further benefit results from the wider, unrestricted movements of the diaphragm and abdominal muscles in that the abdominal organs are consequently subjected to a constant gentle beneficial stimulus resembling a gentle form of massage, thus producing improved circulation in these organs. This is particularly beneficial to the liver, which is situated immediately below the diaphragm. When the very important vital activities of the liver are considered – including the processing of nutrients, the breaking down of waste products and other toxins, including drug residues, for excretion via the kidneys – it may be more easily appreciated how beneficial these self-help treatments may be.

For all these reasons the exercises and instructions in this and the following chapter should be practised assiduously and the reader should subsequently proceed to incorporate these principles and practices into his or her way of life.

The following exercises are designed to free stiffened joints of the ribs and thoracic spine and the shoulder girdle, increasing the range of movement for deeper breathing and increased lung capacity.

Exercise 2 (see illustration on p. 132)

Sideways-bending stretch   Seated on a straight-backed chair or stool, feet apart, clasp the hands together on top of the head. Bend the trunk sideways to the right while pulling sideways and downwards with the right arm to increase the bending movement until strong tension is felt on the left ribs. Hold this position while taking a strong, deep breath, then exhale fully while returning to the starting position. Repeat the exercise, bending to the left.

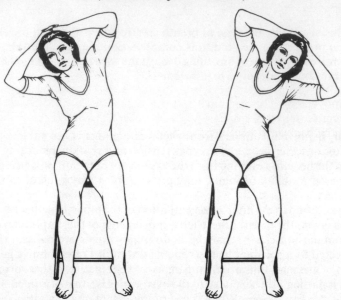

Exercise 3 (see illustration below)

Rotation   Sitting astride a stool, stretch the arms out sideways at shoulder level, then swing them so that the body rotates with the arms to the right as far as possible. The whole trunk, with the head and neck, should take part in this smooth movement. Then swing as far as possible to the left in the same manner. Repeat from six to ten times. In this movement the head and neck should turn so as to look as far as possible over each shoulder in turn.

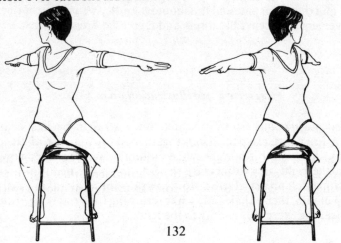

Exercise 4 *(see illustration below)*

Forward bending Sitting on a straight-backed chair, clasp both hands behind the neck, with the elbows to the front and close together. Bend forward from the neck down, pulling with the arms to increase the movement. This will have a stretching effect on the spine and the associated muscles, including the intercostals. Follow immediately with the backward-bending exercise No. 5.

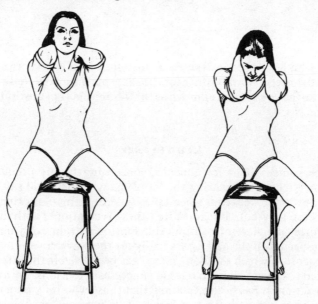

Exercise 5 *(see illustration on p. 134)*

Lie face down on the floor or some other firm surface, with the feet together and the palms of the hands on the floor close to the shoulders. Slowly raise the head, then the neck, raising the trunk upwards and backwards as far as possible assisted by gradual partial straightening of the arms while breathing in deeply. In this exercise the body from the waist down together with the legs should remain on the floor and not be kept stiff as in the familiar press-up exercise, which has an entirely different purpose. Hold for a moment, then return to the starting position while exhaling completely. Repeat once or twice, or more as long as the exercise is not found to be painful or unduly strenuous.

133

Those who have been instructed in yoga may be able to perform the more advanced Cobra Posture for the same purpose as exercise No. 5. Likewise the yoga posture known as the Plough may be substituted for exercise No. 4.

Learn to relax

Further, some explanation is needed concerning the interpretation of the word 'relax'. On hearing the word many readers will say, 'I get relaxation at the weekends when I play golf (or tennis or football, etc., as the case may be).' But too often these recreational activities are performed in a state of considerable tension ('strain every nerve to win'), especially if the game goes badly for the player.

The sense in which the word 'relax' has been used in this chapter is intended to indicate how to release unnecessary tensions, both at rest and in action. It has been explained that those who fully understand how to relax may conserve as much as 30 per cent of their energy compared with that expended in a state of nervous tension. The ability to relax well should ensure that we enjoy restful sleep or, if awake, be enabled to rest completely. *But we also need the ability to relax in activity.* Thus the weekend sportsman may need to relax to improve his game and so liberate his reflexes from frustrating nervous tension.

The reader may obtain further help in these respects from the book *Relax Your Way to Health* by Harold D. Cotton (Thorsons Publishers Ltd).

In addition to specific exercises as above, everyone should cultivate a habit of regular exercise. Walking and swimming are ideal. Where lower limbs are affected discretion is indicated but even the more advanced cases can, with care and patience, gradually increase distance and speed according to ability if the treatment is faithfully carried out.

Hands, elbows, shoulders, feet, knees, hip-joints, etc. should be moved through their maximum range of movement every day, attempting to gain increased movement as treatment progresses.

For those capable of more active exercise care is clearly indicated to avoid overdoing it. Inflamed joints should be moved every day but should not be subjected to inadvisable stress. In these conditions a graduated degree of stress, if not excessive, may be helpful in conjunction with the nutritional plan and with hydrotherapy as described in preceding chapters (also see pp. 163–5).

CHAPTER 18

Relief of Stress, Improved Posture, and Freer Movement

The complex structures and functions of the spine are described, as are the reasons why it does not stand up well to the stresses of civilization, hence the prevalence of backache and certain other ills.

Most people tend to think of the performance of exercises in terms of muscle-building. In dealing with rheumatic conditions, particularly arthritis, the main objective is to ensure the fullest possible range of joint movement with the minimum of painful symptoms. In addition, the exercises we have given are beneficial to the associated muscles which are being alternately stretched and contracted.

Exercises Nos 2–5 described in the previous chapter embody these principles for mobilising the ribs and thoracic spine in order to improve breathing. The other regions of the spine should also be specifically treated, particularly as it is recognised that the spine is one of the first parts of the body to suffer from degenerative changes.

Arthritis in the spine is termed *spondylitis* in its acute stage, while the chronic degenerative states are termed *spondylosis*. A brief description of the structure and functions of the spine will serve to explain the purposes and logical basis of natural treatment.

Look after your spine

The human spine, the backbone, is possibly nature's finest piece of engineering. To the layman its functional characteristics are largely unknown, and even by the medical profession they are relatively neglected until degenerative changes appear to have reached the stage where surgery may be the only recourse. The backbone is, of course, not a single bone but a collection of bones, usually twenty-six in number. Figure 8 illustrates a sideways view of the spine. The top group of seven bones (vertebrae) is known as the *cervical spine*. The next twelve vertebrae are termed the *thoracic* or *dorsal spine*, which with the ribs and breastbone (the *sternum*) form the *thoracic cage*. Below these is the *lumbar spine*, consisting of five vertebrae. Below these again is the large triangular bone called the *sacrum* and finally the 'tail-bone' or *coccyx*.

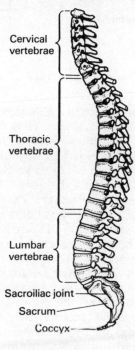

Cervical
vertebrae

Thoracic
vertebrae

Lumbar
vertebrae

Sacroiliac joint

Sacrum

Coccyx

8   The spine

The upper vertebrae are small, and they increase in size down to the sacrum, which is the largest spinal bone. The sacrum articulates with each side of the pelvis through the large L-shaped *sacroiliac joints*, thus transferring the weight of the upper part of the body to the legs.

A few further facts concerning the spine may enable the reader to appreciate how essential it is to preserve the spine with its supporting muscles, tendons and ligaments. (Its main features are illustrated in Figures 8, 9 and 10.)

137

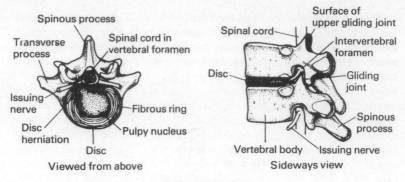

Viewed from above — Sideways view

9 and 10   The spine

The economy of nature is such that almost every structure or organ of the body has more than one function. Thus, first, the spine supports the structure of the body in such a way as to allow a considerable range of movement in many directions. This flexibility is achieved largely with the aid of the *intervertebral discs,* which are inserted between each pair of vertebrae throughout the spine. The discs also buffer the spine, acting as cushions to absorb shocks. The total space occupied by the discs is about one-quarter the length of the spine.

A typical vertebra is illustrated in Figure 9 (above), with the disc resting on the vertebral body, behind which is a bony arch having three projections named *processes*. The latter are very important mechanisms, being the levers to which are attached the muscles which control spinal movements – forward, backward, sideways-bending, rotatory, etc. Figure 10 (above) shows two adjacent vertebrae, side view. The bony arch surrounds a central cavity which (Figure 9) forms a continuous tunnel from one end of the spine to the other, through which runs the spinal cord, normally secure in the protection afforded by this long, bony *spinal canal.*

The spinal cord is, in fact, an extension of the brain with its millions of nerve cells and nerve fibres. The spinal cord leaves the base of the skull and passes through an aperture about the size of a 10p coin to enter the spinal canal. As the cord passes down the spinal canal, nerve branches emerge between each pair of vertebrae (Figures 9 and 10 above), each nerve containing a great number of fibres to be distributed to all parts of the body. Some fibres convey the sense of pain, some the sense of pressure and others of touch, heat, cold, etc., to the brain. Others again – the motor nerves – initiate and control muscle movements according to messages transmitted from the brain or spinal reflexes.

138

Thus, the second function of the spine is to house and protect the spinal cord and its extensions, ensuring the integrity and safe distribution of the nerves without which other functions of the body would cease to operate. In Figure 10 (p. 138), one of the nerves is shown diagramatically emerging from the spine through a small slot-like aperture called the *intervertebral foramen,* situated between two adjoining vertebrae. It will be observed that immediately behind the slot there is a joint. There are four of these joint facets, commonly known as the 'gliding joints', to each vertebra – one upper and one lower on each side of the spine. They serve to stabilise and control the spinal movements in conjunction with muscles and ligaments. Obviously, the size of the slot will alter slightly with the various movements of the spine.

Muscles and Ligaments

All these bony structures are connected by ligaments and muscles, which not only control spinal movements but also give support and check excessive or abnormal movement. From Figures 9 and 10 it will be observed that as the spinal nerve emerges it is in very close proximity to the gliding joint on one side and the disc on the other. The discs are firmly attached to the bodies of the vertebrae above and below and are stabilised also by very strong ligaments in front and behind.

In addition to the nerves, the intervertebral foramena accommodate blood-vessels (veins and arteries) and lymphatic vessels, which enter and leave the spine so as to provide nutrition to and drainage from all the spinal tissues.

A third function of the spinal bones is the production of new blood cells in the bone marrow. Damage or destruction of these blood-forming elements may result in a form of anaemia. A number of drugs, including anti-rheumatic drugs, are known to cause this condition, which in some cases may be fatal. Faulty nutrition also may be responsible for loss of these blood-forming tissues.

Unfortunately, the civilised spine is subject to a number of troubles, almost all of which are directly due to one or other form of rheumatism or arthritis or at least have a rheumatic basis. It has been stated that in this country alone more than one and a half million sufferers from back pain seek medical aid annually, and this is almost certainly only the tip of the iceberg. It has often been said, also, that such troubles are largely due to the upright human posture, assuming that our early ancestors went on all fours. This is a questionable hypothesis for among our domestic quadrupeds certain forms of arthritis and spinal weakness are not unknown, even though their lifespan is comparatively short. On the other hand, photographs that have been taken of healthy and long-living remote primitives, such as the Hunza and the Caucasians, show remarkable freedom from spinal weakness. They are seen to be active and their posture remains upright even at the age of a hundred or more. A further example has more recently come to light with an isolated community in Ecuador.

The truth is that the human spine is durable and efficient if it is well nourished with natural nutrients and well used. If the spine becomes a weak and unstable structure, it is almost certainly due to the weakening and degenerative habits and polluted environment of our modern civilisation. Without much difficulty we may define the principle causes of weakness and malfunction. The enervating and eventually destructive results of faulty nutrition, shallow breathing, nervous tension, the toxic products of industrial chemistry and in particular the torrent of drugs have already been described. To these must be added the lack of regular exercise and also occupational stresses.

Faulty Posture

A further widespread and constant factor is faulty posture, which, in many people, will be aggravated by the burden of excess weight due to defective dietary. All these factors combine to undermine the integrity of the spine, making the eventual onset of spinal arthritis virtually certain unless positive steps are taken to counteract the cumulative effects of the various stress factors, including faulty posture.

The first step towards the restoration of the mechanical integrity of the spine and the correction of bad posture is to restore as fully as possible the mobility of the spinal joints.

In the thoracic spine, the regular practice of exercises Nos 1–5 for deeper breathing is effective in restoring the freedom of movement in the thoracic vertebrae and ribs. In addition, the following exercises will be effective in mobilising the neck vertebrae and the lower spine. It is usually helpful to view oneself in a mirror while performing the exercises.

Exercise No. 6 (see illustration on p. 141)

The sideways-bending (as in exercise No. 2) may be applied to the lumbar region by standing with the feet about 18 inches apart. While holding the arms straight close to the sides, slide one hand down towards the knee while keeping both knees straight. Come back to the erect position and repeat on the other side. This exercise will stretch the muscles on one side of the lumbo-sacral spine and contract those on the other side and vice versa, and it thus serves to mobilise the joints while strengthening their supporting structures. Repeat from six to eight times.

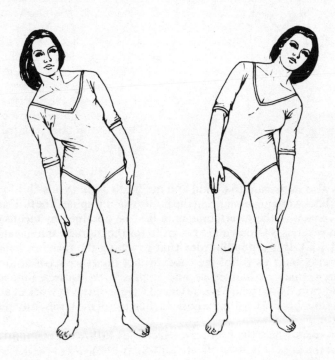

Exercise No. 7 (see illustration on p. 142)

While remaining standing with the feet apart exercise No. 3 (p. 132), raise the arms straight sideways to shoulder level and swing the whole body in a circular movement to the farthest possible point of rotation, first to right and then to left. Rotation in the lumbar spine is limited, but such movement as there is should be achieved and maintained.

141

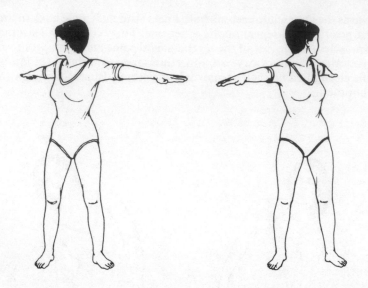

It is also important to obtain and maintain as far as possible forward and backward movements in the lumbo-sacral spine. The full range of movement of these vertebrae may best be obtained by means of the same exercises (Nos 4 and 5) as given for the thoracic spine (pages 131 and 132). It is a popular idea that touching the toes is a beneficial exercise, but this is not the case; in fact in arthritic conditions this exercise may be dangerous and it may even cause a slipped disc condition. Those who have observed weight-lifters at work at athletic meetings or on TV will have noticed their use of the knees to avoid back strain.

In cases where the knees are affected by arthritis it is important to treat the knee condition effectively (see p. 163).

At the base of the spine the large triangular sacrum articulates with the pelvic bones through the sacroiliac joints. These joints, which have large, somewhat irregular surfaces resembling an inverted 'L', are among the most important weight-bearing joints of the body. They have normally a small but very important degree of mobility which is retained and supported by very strong ligaments and muscles. Sacroiliac strains with minor displacements and fixations in this region may be very painful, and the resulting inflammatory rheumatic condition which may result is termed *sacroillitis*. It may be a major factor in causing disc lesions ('slipped discs'), which are very prevalent in all modern civilised societies. If not effectively treated, these dis-

142

orders of the lower lumbar and pelvic joints are likely to develop into a progressive increasing condition of osteoarthritis.

In many cases of arthritis some form of trauma has been involved, such as lifting strains, falls, car accidents, etc., but in others sudden onset occurs with severe pain without there being any known traumatic incident. In either instance the causes are *multifactorial*. Poor-quality nutrition producing poor-quality tissues, which are lacking in tensile strength, and abnormal conditions of the blood have been found in association with rheumatic diseases, and no doubt there are other changes in the very complex body fluids (blood, lymph and tissue fluid) which have not so far been identified. Further deterioration in the quality and tensile strength of muscles and other vital tissues may result from insufficient exercise and the long-term effect of postural stresses superimposed upon weakened tissues.

In its endeavour to maintain the essential balance of homoeostasis the body resorts to the secondary defence mechanisms of fever and inflammation, mucus discharges, skin rashes and other efforts in order to rid the system of accumulated toxic residues which are overloading the normal channels of elimination.

The orthodox treatments with suppressive drugs may merely mask the symptoms while heat treatments are rapidly going out of fashion because it is realised that they are rarely helpful and in some cases may be harmful. Surgical corsets stiffen already restricted joints, weaken supportive muscles and restrict breathing. Mechanical traction may exacerbate, and will rarely correct, joint lesions.

In addition to the exercises Nos 1–7 the following two exercises will assist in resolving the mechanical factors in lumbo-sacral lesions.

Exercise No. 8 (see illustration on p. 144)

Stand at arm's length from a wall or door or mantelshelf with the feet together and the arms horizontal, with the palms on the wall, door or shelf. For a left-sided lumbo-sacral lesion extend the right leg backwards so that, with the toes on the ground and both knees straight, it is not quite possible, by stretching, to press the heel to the floor. Then, slowly and firmly, press down the right heel until it touches the floor. While in this position, alternately press and release the right foot about six times. In this way you will alternately stretch and release all the muscles from the calf through the back of the thigh as well as those on one side of the lumbar spine, up to the points of attachment to the lower ribs.

143

Return the right leg to the starting position and repeat the process with the left leg.

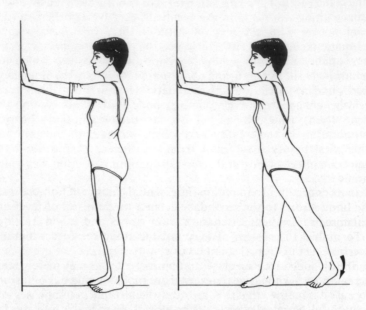

Exercise No. 9 (see illustration below)

For mobilising the sacroiliac joint Lying on the back on the floor or some other firm surface, raise one leg, bending the knee and the thigh up towards the abdomen as completely as possible. With the heel lightly resting on the floor, drop the bent leg outwards, then straighten it and lower to the floor.

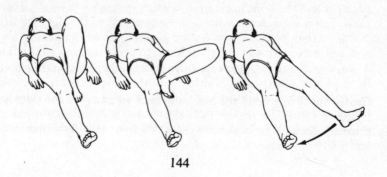

Equally important is the mechanical integrity of the upper dorsal and cervical spine. These structures, perhaps more than any others, are subject to the effects of nervous tension and faulty posture, but before either of these conditions can be fully corrected it is necessary to ensure freedom of movement of the many joints involved.

Many people realise that these movements are limited only when they experience difficulty, and probably pain, on attempting to look at the ceiling or the sky above or, in the case of car drivers, in turning the head when reversing.

They may also experience giddiness in performing such movements. Even worse, it may be that just as *lumbago* and *sciatica* may result from lumbo-sacral strains and rheumatic changes, so in the cervical and upper dorsal region the condition known as *brachial neuritis* may arise. This may cause pain and sensations of numbness in the shoulders, arms or hands; in fact, a very large proportion of all headaches may be due to the presence of rheumatism in the cervical and upper dorsal joints, possibly also involving disc lesions, perhaps diagnosed as *cervical spondylitis.*

To mobilise the joints of the neck, including the upper thoracic vertebrae, the following exercises should be carried out gently and smoothly, but with increasing firmness as the range of movements increases. Each should be repeated from six to ten times.

Exercise No. 10 (see illustration on p. 146)

Turn the head and neck fully to the right as if trying to look over the shoulder and down the back, but without turning the shoulders. At the limit of each movement press as if trying to rotate farther. Return to the front and repeat the movement to the left.

Exercise No. 11 (see illustration on p. 146)

Gently but firmly bend the head and neck sideways to the right as if trying to touch the ear on to the shoulder but without raising the shoulder. Repeat, bending sideways to the left, pressing in each case in an effort to increase the limit of movement.

Illustration of Exercise No. 11

Exercise No. 12 (see illustration below)

This exercise is important both for freeing joints and correcting posture, in association with the special posture-correcting exercise No. 15. It is particularly important that this movement is performed in front of a mirror. Looking at your image in the mirror, make sure that the head is not tilted backward, then push the head as far forward as possible and immediately move it as far backward as possible, again ensuring that the head is not tilted backward (i.e. avoid a nodding movement). This has the effect of moving the gliding joints of the spinal vertebrae forwards and backwards over each other. To ensure good posture, this exercise must finish at the point where the chin is comfortably tucked in towards the chest.

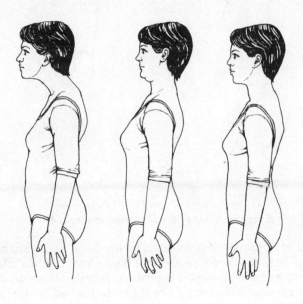

Exercise No. 13 (see illustration below)

Raise and lower both shoulders together toward the ears, then continue in a circular movement when viewed from the side, rotating about six times in clockwise and six in anticlockwise movement.

Exercise No. 14 (see illustration on p.149)

The last of this series of exercises is forward and backward bending. Bend the head forward steadily until the chin touches the chest, and then move it up and back as far as possible. In the presence of advanced arthritic changes some care is needed in the backward movement. If this exercise causes giddiness or pain or numbness or tingling in the hands or arms, the movement should be limited accordingly. By concentrating mainly on the other neck exercises at first, the range of forward and backward movement may be gradually extended, with easing of symptoms, but always in conjunction with nutritional therapy as indicated in earlier chapters.

With all these mobilising exercises the objectives should be achieved by adding gentle but firm additional pressure at the end of each movement. The cervical and dorsal exercises may be performed while seated, preferably on a firm stool or bench seat, if the neck movements have any tendency to produce giddiness. The same consideration applies to the following method of postural correction.

Correct Your Posture

It is hardly possible to exaggerate the importance of correct posture in all aspects of sitting, standing or walking. Bad posture is one of the most common characteristics of civilised people, and the tendency appears to be increasing among young and old alike. Contributory factors include sedentary occupations from schooldays onwards and the greatly increased use of mechanical transport. With many hours of TV viewing, the inactivity has extended to the leisure hours.

Among the youth of today it would almost seem that drooping, slumpy posture is in fashion. Few of these young people realise the harm that may come to them eventually if they persist in this bad habit. Still less do they associate their postural errors with the back aches, sciaticas, migraines, brachial neuritis and the development of

149

fibrositis fatigue, arthritis and other ailments from which so many are suffering. The reasons for these injurious habits may be partly psychological, possibly a reaction to the old military concept of rigid 'stand to attention'.

The objective should be a posture which is upright yet easy, relaxed and well balanced. For this reason we may say that the first rule of posture is, *'it must be easy',* for any habitual posture that is 'held' with tension and any degree of rigidity *must* be faulty and potentially harmful.

Exercise No. 15 (for postural correction)

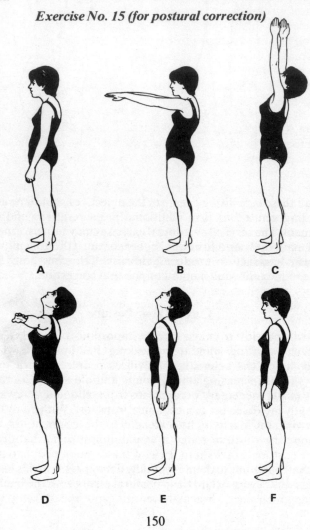

A   B   C

D   E   F

Thus, traditional instructions from parents, teachers and even in some cases physical training instructors to 'pull yourself up', or to 'think tall', or 'pull your shoulders back' are all contrary to the basic rule of 'straight and easy' (see p. 129).

In this respect, the following exercise has proved of great value. It is a corrective exercise which should not be confused with those of the Swedish-drill type. The essential difference lies in the way the movement is carried out, so that to achieve the desired result the instructions should be observed carefully, stage by stage.

In cases where rheumatic conditions have already led to restriction of movement, stiffness and some degree of joint fixation, particular attention must be given to exercises Nos 9–14 in conjunction with the other spinal exercises and the advised nutritional plan in order to obtain maximum freedom of the affected joints. If, in addition, the services of a qualified naturopath and osteopath may be obtained his help may be invaluable.

Figure A illustrates the common postural fault. The neck is seen to be sloping forward at about 30° or more from the vertical. Thus, the head has to be tilted back in relation to the neck in order to face forwards. This results in constant tension of the muscles at the back of the neck (a possible cause of headaches). Note the rounded back and the hollow curve at the waist, with resulting flattening of the chest and protrusion of the abdomen, predisposing to backaches and sagging of the abdominal organs.

Figure F illustrates the corrected posture, with the neck vertical, the dorsal and lumbar curves restored to normal, the chest erect and the abdomen flattened. Most important, the resulting posture is balanced, effortless, relaxed and easy.

The wearing of high-heeled shoes as in women's fashionable footwear obviously distorts the whole posture and may be a cause of backache by distortion of the lumbar spine and pelvis in addition to damaging the feet. Women should be aware of these dangers. There may, indeed, be a case for representations to be made to footwear manufacturers to modify their designs of footwear so as to avoid inflicting such damage on those who wear this form of footwear at the dictate of fashion.

The stages from A to F are performed as follows:

1   Starting from the faulty posture of Figure A with feet parted a few inches for stability and hands to sides, steadily raise the stretched arms forward and up to the horizontal *position B*.

151

2   With the eyes watching the fingertips, continue to raise the stretched arms steadily to the vertical position while tilting the head and neck steadily backwards in phase with the movement of the arms, thus reaching the *position C*. By maintaining the stretching of the arms the reader will feel that he or she is 'reaching strongly towards the ceiling'. Note that the trunk should *not be bent backwards,* the movement being confined to the arms, head and neck. The eyes then will be looking towards the ceiling.

3   Keeping the head and neck in the same position facing the ceiling, looking straight upwards, the arms, still stretched, are steadily lowered outwards and downwards to *position D* and then to lie loosely to the sides as in *position E,* while the head and neck remain unmoved. At this point *drop the shoulders.* This latter is a very important point, for at this stage most people are found to have the shoulders to some extent raised and therefore not relaxed.

4   The final movement is to bring the head forwards, looking to the front as in the final position, *position F,* which should feel relaxed and easy.

While walking, if this easy, balanced posture is maintained, all the movements will be felt to be easy and relaxed and performed with the minimum of effort.

This whole exercise should be performed slowly and evenly, occupying about thirty seconds, with a brief pause at each stage. It is advisable to perform the exercise in front of a mirror so that visual observation may supplement the sensory appreciation and thus, with repetition, to consciously instil the concept, the 'feel' and the habit of correct posture. The whole exercise should be repeated at least two or three times daily until the correct postural habit has become instinctive.

Not only in standing and walking but also in sitting, working at a bench, desk, kitchen sink, etc., or when reading, knitting or in similar occupations the same relationship of the neck in line with the trunk should be preserved, with the chin neatly tucked in towards the chest. Also forward bending should primarily involve only movement from hips and knees and so without disturbing the neck–head–trunk relationship.

The postural correction exercise may also be practised while seated, thus ensuring correct sitting posture. Elderly sufferers from rheumatism may in fact find it easier to practise the exercise while seated on a stool or straight chair.

Incidentally, domestic furniture often imposes faulty posture, causing strains in the spine and muscles. Thus it is advisable to avoid slumpy chairs and saggy or over-soft beds, when the insertion of a hard board under the mattress may be helpful. The board should go full width across the bed and be about 4'6" long.

While the suggested corrective exercises are helpful in most cases, especially when practised regularly, there is in addition the need for regular active exercise such as walking, swimming and also, according to age and condition, more lively and energetic forms of activity, possibly including games such as tennis, badminton, squash, or other forms of active exercise that induce lively, deep breathing and stimulate the circulation.

Common sense should dictate reasonable care to avoid undue stress being imposed on arthritic joints, but as improvement is gained unexpected possibilities may open up in many cases.

Walking should at first be limited by the same considerations, with distance and pace being gradually increased according to progress. Thus, while in the acute phase of arthritis rest may be essential, as inflammation is reduced by means of the measures here advised a suitable plan of increasing exercise and activity should be undertaken.

Sufferers from rheumatism and arthritis should be aware of the possible dangers of sunbathing. Overexposure to summer sun may possibly worsen rather than improve their condition. Each spring warnings are given of this possible danger. To begin with, no more than a ten-minute exposure is advisable, gradually increasing to about twenty minutes at most, and somewhat less for those who have very fair skins. Remember that the most potent rays are the invisible ultra-violet. These are not heat rays and they readily penetrate light cloud. Also cooling breezes may be deceptive.

Remember also that the fashionable tanning of the skin does not indicate health. It is the pigment produced by the body in an effort to resist overexposure, far more than is needed in order to obtain sufficient of the sunshine-vitamin D.

Similar considerations and warnings of possible harm apply also to the use of ultraviolet-ray sun-lamps, which, if used at all, should be under professional supervision. Gross over-exposure to ultraviolet rays or to sun may be a cause of skin cancer.

CHAPTER 19

The Body-mind Relationship, Self-help, and Adaptation

The Principle of wholeness applies particularly to the body-mind relationship, and because both mind and body are involved in negative mental-emotional states treatment is described which has proved effective in very many cases of anxiety, depression and other negative emotional states.

As mentioned in an earlier chapter the principle of wholeness implies that in both sickness and health the body and the mind cannot be regarded as being separate entities. Similarly, just as orthodox medicine tends to regard each disease as a separate entity, so there is created a supposed necessity for the establishment of a professional speciality for the treatment of mind and emotions. Hence the psychiatrist, whose view tends to be that most illness originates in the mind, will indicate the need for psychoanalysis (the procedures initiated by Freud), the object of which is to reveal any causes of anxiety and other harmful states of mind.

Many readers will have encountered psychiatric patients who have undergone regular courses of psychoanalysis extending over years without being relieved of their 'complexes'. At least psychiatric treatment aims at revealing natural causes of mental-emotional illness, but as Milton Powell has written, 'As a method of cure it has proved too highly complicated. It involves a fantastic outlay in time, money, effort and patience. Its relative failure, indeed, to cope with the increasing tide of modern psychosis and neurosis is doubtless the main reason why mental specialists so often use such drastic physical methods as electric convulsion therapy, insulin-shock treatment, "truth-drugs" and frontal leucotomy. These sometimes give relief, but usually the last state of the patient is worse than the first.'

None of these methods is in any true sense curative, and violent measures such as electro-convulsive therapy (ECT) and the even more mutilating leucotomy, in which certain fibres of the brain are surgically severed, are procedures of a dubious ethical nature which have been subject to severe criticism from within the medical profession, particularly among the higher medical authorities.

Thus, Professor Thomas Szasz, Professor of Psychiatry at the State University of New York in Syracuse, is quoted (*New Scientist and Science Journal,* 3 June 1971) as saying in an interview that 'Mental illness is not an illness. Although there have been advances in psychiatric medicine in the past 25 years, such as the discovery of certain chemical tranquillising and stimulant treatments, the advances are not all that impressive.' The professor added: 'People recover spontaneously from complex disorders in about the same number as those who have had treatments. There is nothing organically wrong with people who are diagnosed as mentally ill. They may be confused or distressed or behaving very oddly, but they are not ill in the way someone who has something physically wrong with him or who has measles or a myocardial infarction is ill.'

Professor Szasz also discussed the ethics of psychiatry saying, 'Although there has been much discussion recently about the ethics of medical interventions, such as transplants, there has been surprisingly little argument about the ethics of psychiatry. For instance, people are subjected to very violent treatments such as electro-shock therapy. Yet there are few objectors – and those tend to be from very radical psychiatrists.'

In spite of such criticism the fact is that the psychiatrist's couch, with its implication of personal contact between doctor and patient, is now virtually discarded with few exceptions, and instead the treatment of anxiety and other forms of neurosis is 'Drugs by the Million', as headlined by one national daily paper. The brain – the most delicate, complex and sensitive biological mechanism in the world – is being assailed, its activity repeatedly stimulated by antidepressant drugs (pep pills), suppressed by tranquillizers and an artificial form of sleep enforced by narcotic drugs ('sleeping pills').

Anxiety Neurosis Increasing

One reason for the changes in the forms of treatment for anxiety neurosis, etc., is that the number of sufferers from these complaints has risen enormously. This was disclosed in an address by Dr William Sargant to the World Psychiatric Association Conference, in which he stated: 'Whether we like it or not, and even if we think that many of the millions of sufferers from anxiety all over the world should preferably be treated on analytic couches, by individual psychotherapy, by the alteration of what is often an unalterable environment, *it is by the use of drugs* [my italics – C.Q.] . . . that the vast majority are going to have to be treated in actual practice.' He added: 'However, some patients

155

would be helped by drugs only at the expense of increasing addiction and deterioration.'

The *Guardian* (14 November, 1967), reporting on the Conference under the headline 'Drugs by the Million to Keep Anxiety at Bay', referred to our present state as 'A Drug-dependent Culture'.

In contrast with this, it is well to realise that in the more primitive communities mentioned earlier in this book anxiety appears to be non-existent.   Professor Szasz's statement concerning the nature of mental illness makes sense only if we remember that the concept of diseases as being separate entities is basically fallacious and may lead to erroneous ideas of treatment. Anxiety neuroses are originally functional disturbances which may affect to greater or lesser extent, directly or indirectly, the normal workings of any or every organ or system of the body, possibly affecting, for instance, heart-rate, breath-rate, blood circulation, sexual activity, and bowel and urinary function, and they may even affect clarity of vision and possibly cause loss of balance. Such functional stresses naturally tend to disturb the essential balance of homoeostasis, and, if they persist, they may lead to some form of organic disease.

The Third Factor

Thus, while physical causes of rheumatism and arthritis such as faulty metabolism, dietary errors and obvious factors of mechanical stress, together with the accumulation of toxic residues, and worsened by faulty elimination, may all be appreciated, the importance of the third factor of disease causation mental-emotional disturbance must not be overlooked or minimised (see pp. 166–7).

From what has been written, readers should be able to appreciate that the concept of a 'magic bullet' to 'knock out' rheumatism and arthritis is quite illogical and deceptive. On the other hand, it is logical and essential to accept the necessity of understanding that, however much others may endeavour to help the sufferer, *there is an absolute need for self-help* in order to eliminate the physical causes of these diseases and to build positive health. Otherwise, it is a fallacy to speak of 'cure' in any real sense of the word. Absence of pain alone may be merely temporary and may not necessarily mean that the condition is cured.

It may, however, be much more difficult to appreciate how the mental-emotional causes of illness are to be understood, defined and resolved by processes of self-help, especially considering that these factors and their workings may be deeply rooted in the processes of the subconscious mind.

Personal Involvement Needed

The fact is that little or no progress is likely to be achieved in this respect without realising the absolute need for personal involvement in solving these psychological problems. Fortunately, this may not be as difficult as it may at first appear. How this desirable objective may be approached and eventually attained requires some further explanation. First, it may be enlightening if the usual medical approach and its possible effects on the patient's mental outlook are briefly considered.

Very many sufferers visiting the doctor because of aches and pains, possibly allied to a general sense of 'not feeling well', and already somewhat depressed and perhaps not a little anxious, are likely to experience a further sense of depression resulting from the advice so generally given by orthodox medical practitioners. Symptoms are medically classified in two categories. Those which are observable by the doctor are termed *objective symptoms,* and those numerous symptoms which are perceptible only to the sufferer are termed *subjective symptoms.* In many instances, the earlier symptoms of rheumatism and arthritis are mostly *subjective* – perhaps pains which may be intermittent and move from one part to another. Almost certainly, a prescription will be given on a symptomatic basis, and with almost equal certainty side-effects will appear to cause further malaise, possibly including feelings of nausea, digestive disturbances, loss of appetite and perhaps headaches, etc.

The doctor may consider such side-effects as these to be 'acceptable', but in the patient they may increase anxiety, either conscious or subconscious. Many patients with mainly subjective symptoms, perhaps also with side-effects of drugs, may eventually be referred for psychiatric treatment (on the assumption that their troubles may be all, or at least partly, 'in the mind'), only to be treated with more pills. In this event the patient is well justified in feeling anxious and depressed. The final word from the doctor may then be, 'There is no cure for rheumatism or arthritis,' followed by, 'Try to learn to live with it, and keep on taking the pills.'

A Vicious Circle

Naturally, as a result of the doctor's verdict the already existing state of anxiety and depression may worsen, an example of 'body affecting mind' to be followed by 'mind reacting on body' – truly a vicious circle.

This also reveals some of the pitfalls of medical overspecialisation. The psychologist or psychiatrist may be mainly, if not solely,

157

concerned with the effects of mind on body, with little interest in the reverse process, while the GP will regard psychology as not being within his field of study. Consequently, the patient's anxiety is deepened rather than relieved.

A further possible cause of fear, confusion and anxiety may arise due to pains in the chest or abdomen which, although intermittent, may be severe and may simulate the pains of *angina pectoris* or even of organic disease of heart, lungs, bowels, etc. Even after extensive medical tests the doctor may fail to find organic disease, but his reassurance may not succeed in allaying the patient's fears if the pains persist. Here again, the patient may be judged to be a case for psychiatric treatment, which in turn is unlikely to be successful. The patient is thus left with both the pains and the unrelieved anxiety.

There is rarely any mention of these referred pains in medical literature. In the absence of organic disease such pains may be due solely to rheumatic conditions in the joints of the ribs, spine or sternum, or to fibrositis in the associated muscular and connective tissues. However, in one instance Dr Frank L. Raney, Jr, in addressing the 33rd annual meeting of the American Academy of Orthopaedic Surgeons at Chicago, said: 'Pain arising from derangement of rib-joints can mimic pain from other sources and thereby simulate a number of conditions such as appendicitis, duodenal ulcer, coronary insufficiency and unexplained abdominal pain.' In such events, if the natural treatments already described have been carried out thoroughly and persistently, such pains when due to *intercostal neuritis* should have disappeared or at least be greatly eased, much to the relief of the person concerned. If such pains are still not completely resolved it may be helpful to obtain the services of a qualified naturopath and osteopath who should be able to correct any joint and soft tissue osteopathic lesions that may be associated with such symptoms.

Physical Self-help aids Mental Stress

Thus the measures of physical self-help already expounded, if carried out with thoroughness and perseverance, will provide the best possible first steps towards successful psychotherapy. With the health-giving plan of whole-food nutrition, plus the adoption of methods to improve body mechanics, including better posture and deeper breathing, helping to establish more efficient elimination of toxic waste matter, all these will contribute towards an increasing sense of well-being and relief from harmful factors of stress, both mental and physical.

All this will be more successful if progress has been achieved in the art of relaxation, correcting and relieving old habits of nervous tension by means of the exercises described for this purpose in an earlier chapter. It should be noted that whereas orthodox psychotherapy is mainly concerned with psychosomatic (mind-body) conditions, naturopathy is particularly concerned with somatico-psychic (body-mind) relationships in disease causation, particularly concerning the influence of natural physical therapy helping in creating a more healthy and positive attitude of mind. In this respect it is necessary to distinguish between the physical nervous system, as described in Chapter 8, and the popular usage of the word 'nerves' when, in fact, relating to states of emotion (see pp. 160–1). Factors of stress – nutritional, mechanical or chemical – and in particular the baleful effects of drugs may individually or collectively have weakened, oversensitised and possibly damaged the complex structures of the nervous system.

Only the body's natural, spontaneous powers of healing and repair, actively assisted by methods of natural therapy, will serve to strengthen the weakened and damaged nervous tissues, with similar effects on other parts and organs. The benefits of these physical treatments will thus be to create the conditions which will facilitate the relief of mental-emotional stresses which are frequently a factor in causing, or at least worsening, states of rheumatism and arthritis.

Great as the benefits obtained from the physical treatments may be, problems of mental-emotional stress may remain. In many cases there may be a psychological history of deeply ingrained habits of thought and feelings such as fear, frustration, suppressed rage, resentment or remorse, any or all of which negative emotions may be destructive to health and harmony. Such functional disturbance, if unresolved, may prove to be the third factor in the three main natural causes of disease, sometimes referred to as the 'triad of disease causation' (see p. 89).

Treatment with drugs which cloud the mind and suppress normal sensitivity can seldom if ever resolve these negative mental-emotional reactions. In all but the most severe states of anxiety and nervous tension there is a clear possibility of transforming these negative states into a happier state of thought and feeling. This again calls for a plan of self-help on the part of the sufferer.

How to Help Yourself

To understand how such self-help may be applied successfully there are a few simple facts which should be noted. At the subconscious or the unconscious levels of the mind there is a 'repeater'. Using a computer analogy, as it is 'programmed' so that it will continue to produce the same pattern or behaviour, thought or feeling unless the 'programme' is changed. If this were not an essential property of the mind we would never be able to learn and recall and so would not be able to talk, write or develop skills of any kind.

This attribute of the subconscious mind will be a faithful servant if the repeating pattern is benevolent and helpful but it may be correspondingly harmful if it perpetuates negative, depressive habits of thought and emotion.

Fortunately we are not inevitably bound by our existing behavioural pattern of the subconscious. Harmful, negative mental processes need not always rule our lives. The possibility remains that we may replace the harmful patterns of thought and emotion with more benevolent and health-giving behavioural patterns instilled at both conscious and subconscious levels, thus transforming our whole outlook on life with lasting benefit. The process by which this desirable change may be achieved is well known under the title of auto-suggestion.

The practical method employed in autosuggestion is based on the continuous repetition of the desired new pattern of habitual thought and behaviour, so as to transfer this new pattern via the conscious mind to the subconscious. It is possible to do this in such a manner that the new, desirable habit will erase and replace the older, negative and harmful habits of thought and feeling. In such ways, just as the body possesses its inbuilt natural healing powers, so has the mind its intrinsic powers which may be used to exert favourable, benevolent influences over our mental-emotional processes, much to our present and future contentment and well-being.

Autosuggestion Must be Realistic

If autosuggestion is to be successful it must correspond with reality. For instance, most readers will be familiar with the name of Émile Coué, the French psychologist who promoted a system aimed at self-improvement by means of autosuggestion in which the patient would constantly repeat the words: 'Day by day and in every way I am getting better and better.' This idea caught on, for it seemed to be an easy way to improvement if this regular assertion proved sufficient to cure mental ills. Unfortunately, it is not difficult to imagine the disillusionment which will eventually follow such a mechanical form of autosuggestion if other necessary measures to resolve the basic causes of ill health, both mental and physical, are neglected so that the suggestion fails to correspond with reality. But if, on the other hand, the programme of treatment by means of natural therapy has been followed, a well justified plan of autosuggestion may be adopted with lasting benefit. Thus, in addition to physical improvement, negative emotional states and nervous tension may be discharged to be replaced by happier thoughts and feelings and with new confidence in the present and the future.

A further way in which it is necessary to be realistic is to accept that the path to better health is rarely uniformly smooth. Dr Bertrand Allinson, when speaking at a public meeting, was asked by one member of his audience, 'Do you consider that nature cure performs miracles?' Dr Allinson replied, 'Yes, Nature Cure can perform slow miracles.' In other words, the wonderful processes of natural healing and repair generally require a time factor however we may strive to hasten them – hence the need for patience and perseverance.

Thus, while in some rheumatic cases progress may be comparatively rapid and uneventful, others may experience continuing discomfort for a time or even what may appear to be a temporary worsening before marked improvement supervenes. Some of nature's most effective defensive and curative reactions, such as inflammation, catarrhal and other discharges, and in some cases rheumatic skin rashes, may cause temporary discomforts, but even in severe cases signs of positive improvement will become evident. In any or all of these events the sufferer should exercise appropriate patience and perseverence.

With physical progress bringing a sense of present relief, and with a more hopeful and happy mental outlook, an appropriate personal programme of autosuggestion will be realistic and should be justified by the establishment of positive helpful thoughts and emotions by means of which previous negative and destructive emotional patterns may cease to be 'repeaters' and so will no longer be able to exert their baleful influence either mental or physical.

Psychologists warn of the hazards of emotional suppression, one of the most dangerous forms of which may result from the use of psychiatric drugs, tranquillisers, sedatives, hypnotics, etc. The methods of self-help described in this book allied to the methods of relaxation explained in Chapter 17, are designed to release suppressed negative thoughts and may prove to be the most valuable and efficient way of discharging such causes of nervous tension and of substituting happier states of positive thought and feeling which will promote the natural healing of both mind and body. A summary of the treatment plan appears as an Appendix.

CHAPTER 20

The Relief of Pain:
Specific Treatments and Aids

Simple hydrotherapy in the home is described, together with specific measures needed in individual cases.

It is emphasised that the programme of nutritional therapy (Chapters 13, 14 and 15) must be carried out in detail, and that the subsequent adoption of a balanced whole-food dietary will promote further progress and help to prevent recurrences.

In Chapter 2 a number of specific forms of rheumatism and arthritis were briefly described and in succeeding chapters it was explained that these various conditions, although labelled with different medical terms, all have certain basic causes arising from our habits of life and factors in our environment.

Hence, while it is imperative that the basic methods of natural treatment must apply in all cases, there are in addition a number of aids which will be helpful in the various forms of rheumatic diseases and in particular those which are directly related to specific joints, muscles, ligaments, tendons, capsules, etc., as in osteoarthritis.

First, let us consider those joints in which the early stages of arthritis are marked with swelling, perhaps reddening and heat, and at some stage pain (the signs of inflammation). It is important to remember that in many cases there is a gradual build-up of pathological changes before the point at which pain is felt. This point has been described as the *threshold* of pain (see pp. 15–16) and if and when the inflammatory reaction has achieved some degree of success the pain may ease, having receded through the threshold. Countless millions of doses of anti-inflammatory drugs, particularly aspirin, are still being consumed. The very cogent objections to the widespread use of these drugs have already been stated, not the least being the frequency of recurrences leading to a chronic state of inflammation and progressively increasing chronic arthritic degeneration, leading eventually to erosion of joint cartilage and bone. The early stages of rheumatism and arthritis may be relatively painless. The point where pain ensues, the threshold, almost invariably recedes under nature cure and in most cases eventually disappears.

Home Hydrotherapy for Reducing Pain

A far superior method of dealing with inflammation in localised areas of joints and muscles is by means of hydrotherapy.

This type of treatment is employed with good effect in nature-cure hydros and health farms, but there are simple forms of hydrotherapy which may be used easily and effectively at home.

Directions for the use of cold compresses in the form of body packs for feverish conditions have been given on p. 120 and the same principle is used for acute arthritic conditions in specific areas such as the knees, shoulders, elbows, etc., and also in areas affected by fibrositis. When correctly applied, the cold compress will be extremely helpful, effectively reducing swelling, easing pain and assisting the success of the curative inflammatory reaction.

In the case of an *arthritic knee,* with or without capsulitis or synovitis, whether caused by trauma or a generalised rheumatic tendency, the compress should be applied using a strip of cotton or linen sheeting, about seven or eight inches (20 cm) wide and long enough to go twice around the affected joint. It should be wrung out in cold water and applied (not dripping) to the knee, and then covered, closely overlapping, with dry woollen material. The latter could be a woollen scarf or the leg part of a long sock after cutting off the foot. A suitable circular woollen knee-cap (*not* the elastic type, which is not made of wool) could be knitted, or it can be made in a wrap-round form secured with poppers or Velcro, the two layers being secured with a few safety pins so as to fit snugly together. Similarly, cold compresses may be used for other joints, such as elbows, wrists, ankles, etc. The first effect of the cold compress is to drive blood from the skin inwards, but if it is applied as instructed, within 10–15 minutes at most there will be a reaction, the pack will become warm and in the course of a few hours it will be dry. It may then be washed out and replaced. The compress may be put on at bedtime and remain in position until morning.

The reason why such compresses are so effective is that they serve to stimulate the circulation of blood and lymph, to relieve congestion of body fluids and stimulate the processes of elimination through greatly increased activity of the pores, with the water in the compress forming a continuous liquid medium through the pores with the subcutaneous fluids. In most instances the relief of pain is quite remarkable; also, there is generally a considerable decrease of swelling.

Alternating Water Treatment

After using the cold compresses for three or four days, it is helpful to

163

use alternating hot and cold water treatment for a similar period: wring out a pad of turkish towelling (or similar material) in hot water (test on the back of the hand to avoid scalding). A smear of vegetable oil over the skin before applying will avoid too much skin reddening. The hot cloth fomentations should be applied, remaining in place for about two minutes, and then be immediately replaced with a similar pad wrung out in cold water. Continue to alternate the hot and cold fomentations, two minutes hot and half a minute cold, for about fifteen minutes, finishing with the cold.

This alternation of hot and cold exerts a sort of 'push-pull' effect on the flow of blood and tissue fluid in the affected area and thus stimulates the circulation. In contrast with this the application of heat alone will bring more blood to the affected area without producing a comparable stimulus to the circulatory flow, (a 'lake' effect as compared with a fast flowing 'stream'). For this reason, although heat alone may feel comforting at the time, heat treatments may do more harm than good.

By all means warm the bed in cold weather, but remove the hot-water bottle or the electric blanket on getting into bed. A well-known orthopaedic surgeon has asked why heat treatments are being used all over Europe at great expense when they are either useless or harmful.

Very hot baths, exceeding 98–99°F (37°C), should be avoided for similar reasons. Once weekly an Epsom salts bath may be taken by adding from 1½–2 lb of the salts to the comfortably warm bath water and lying in it for about fifteen minutes before going to bed. A hot bath should, however, be immediately followed by a cool or cold shower or sponge-down. For the elderly or those whose vitality is low the shower or sponge-down after the bath may be taken tepid.

The medical profession has come to agree with the naturopath that the idea of 'taking a tonic' in the form of medicine is a fallacy and that in fact when stimulants are taken any 'kick' which they may provide is likely to be succeeded by the opposite effect – depression.

The Friction Rub

However, there is a very safe and beneficial form of stimulus, with an excellent tonic effect, which should be carried out daily whenever possible, preferably on rising. Using a rough towel, flesh brush or friction gloves, give the trunk, arms and legs a brisk, dry friction rub, taking care to avoid any sore or inflamed areas. Follow immediately with a wet rub, using a short length of rough towelling wrung out in cold water, then dry off briskly. Those with poor circulation may commence with tepid water over limited areas, gradually getting accustomed to colder water and treating a larger area.

It is significant that increases in the red blood-cell count have resulted from this method of stimulating the skin and underlying tissues. Concerning the possibility of increasing vitality, helpful nutritional supplements may include natural sources of vitamins such as pure fruit and vegetable juices. Likewise, seaweed or kelp, either as tablets or in the form of seaweed jellies, provide a rich natural source of essential minerals, including many of the important trace elements. All these products may be obtained from health food stores.

Rheumatoid arthritis is a severe form of rheumatic disease in which changes in the blood, such as increased viscosity, have been detected. Many joints may be involved, in particular the hands and feet, which may become inflamed and painful, with muscle weakness and, in later stages, wasting of muscles. Moreover, the body's defence mechanism (*immunity reaction*) appears to have gone wrong, causing the body to attack its own structures, the joints in particular. This process is termed *autoimmunity*. In the acute stage doctors may advise using splints to immobilise the joints, but this may result in developing *ankylosis* (the locking of joints). Instead, gentle movements should be used, with care.

Strict adherence to the nutritional programme as prescribed in Chapters 14, 15 and 16, commencing with the short fast of from two to three days, should be observed. Cold-water compresses should be used as described above. For hand and wrist compresses use cotton (not nylon) household gloves. Wring them out in cold water and wear them on the hand and over the wrist, covering them with a woollen glove. Likewise for foot trouble, a woollen sock provides a suitable covering over the double layer of cold, wet (but never dripping) cotton sheeting wrapped around the foot. Such compresses may be applied at bedtime and left on until morning, when the compress should have dried out.

These compresses provide one of the surest ways of reducing inflammation and pain. Likewise, the dietary and short fasts (the latter repeated every two weeks in the acute stage of rheumatoid arthritis) also serve to reduce inflammation and pain. As far as possible rest while fasting.

The affected joints must be gently moved daily as far as possible through the full range of normal movements. As inflammation is reduced the hot- and cold-water treatments may be used alternately, together with the cold compresses.

A further helpful procedure is gentle but firm stroking of the arm and leg muscles above the affected joints. This will help the return flow of venous blood and lymph towards the heart. Aids to reduce strains

165

on affected joints in performing everyday tasks are described in the Epilogue.

When possible, especially in very severe cases, a period of treatment in a nature-cure health resort may well be helpful, following which self-treatment at home must be continued.

One of the best forms of exercise for rheumatic sufferers is swimming, or for non-swimmers, just the movement of the affected joints in water. Some hospitals now have heated pools, and many public swimming-baths reserve certain times for this form of hydrotherapy.

Salt

Mention has already been made of the importance of the balance between the numerous minerals needed by the body (about sixteen so far identified). The one salt we take to a much greater extent than we need is *sodium chloride* (common salt). Many people are reluctant to believe that this substance, so familiar in kitchen and dining-room, can be harmful, but it may be so for several reasons: (1) salt raises the blood pressure; (2) it disturbs the natural balance of mineral salts which is necessary for homeostasis; (3) it may cause water retention with swelling of tissues; (4) it throws an extra burden on kidney function; (5) extra salt intake is bad for rheumatic ailments.

All the sodium chloride we need is present in a balanced dietary of whole, natural foods.

The modern doctor should know these risks, but usually he restricts salt intake only in serious cases, such as heart troubles, high blood pressure, kidney disease, etc.

Ankylosing spondylitis is a comparatively rare form of arthritic disease. Its onset usually begins in the teens or the twenties. In this trouble the metabolism of calcium (the hardening matter of the bones) is in some way disturbed so that solid deposits of calcium compounds are laid down in and around the spinal joints, which thereby become rigid. Deposits may be laid down in other joints also. Attention to dietary and general health on natural cure lines will best help towards adapting to the limitations imposed by this condition.

It may be significant that before the 1914–18 war the disease *rickets* was prevalent in which the bones became deformed through lack of calcium, but after that period, with the discovery of vitamins A and D, rickets virtually disappeared as the children were dosed with concentrated sources of these vitamins in the form of orange juice for vitamins A and C and fish-liver oils for vitamin D – the so-called 'sunshine vitamin'. In addition, many prepared children's foods were

166

'fortified' with vitamins A and D (mainly synthetic forms) and many were submitted to ultraviolet radiation.

In the early 1960s it was realised that high dosage of these vitamins could produce side-effects, with calcium being deposited where it is not wanted. Children's complaints of aches and pains, which may be intermittent, may, unfortunately, be dismissed as 'growing pains' and as such may be disregarded. On the contrary, it is possible, even likely, that these are early signs of juvenile arthritis or some other form of rheumatism. A balanced dietary of whole foods with a minimum or none of the ubiquitous refined carbohydrates (white flour and white sugar products) will preserve the integrity of their bones as well as their teeth and will increase their natural resistance to infection in general. When the reasons are properly explained to them most children will agree to cut down their intake of 'sweeties'.

If aches and pains still persist an osteopathic check-up may be important, possibly saving more serious troubles later on, particularly as youngsters are by no means always immune from the effects of their inevitable rough-and-tumble activities.

As mentioned in Chapter 2 the medical term for arthritis of the spine is *spondylitis*. The use of this distinctive term is understandable, first because of the very large number of joints in the spine, and secondly because of its relationship to the spinal cord and spinal nerve roots, and thirdly because of the proximity of important parts of the autonomic nervous system, as described briefly in Chapter 18 and illustrated in Figures 5 and 6. Thus, with inflammations and restrictions in spinal joints, the spinal nerve roots and the adjacent sympathetic ganglia may be affected, giving rise to various forms of neuritis which may cause severe pain and functional disturbances in the regions served by these nerves.

It should be remembered, also, that these structures may be subjected to additional stress from habits of nervous tension, faulty posture and, in many cases, the encumbrances of superfluous tissue accumulated in the same areas by those who are overweight. These distressing forms of neuritis, named according to the affect region of the spine, are very prevalent. In the *cervical spine* (neck), symptoms include pain, stiffness and restriction of movements associated with some degree of *cervical spondylitis* and frequently recurring headaches, often of the *migraine* type. Reflex effects may include *vertigo* (giddiness) or disturbances of eye-focusing, which are not corrected by spectacles.

The spinal segments at the region where the neck meets the upper back are particularly susceptible to mechanical stresses, and *spondylitis* in these vertebrae may cause *brachial neuritis* (usually on

167

one side only, but sometimes on both). In this condition pains in the neck and shoulders may be severe, increasing with certain movements, and pins-and-needles sensations may radiate down the arm, perhaps to the fingers, with loss of musclar strength and possibly cramps in the muscles. Mechanical causes of these conditions include faulty postural habits at desk or bench, or in domestic or other occupations. Nowadays, the jolts and stresses sustained in motoring are a frequent cause of the whiplash injury which may be severe after an accident. Also, disc protrusion or herniation may be responsible for pressures on brachial nerves. In some cases delayed effects from an accident may appear weeks or months after the event.

For the treatment of *brachial neuritis* the programme of nutritional therapy should be strictly followed, the short fast being particularly important in the acute phase. The alternating hot and cold compresses (pp. 163–4) applied to the upper back, shoulder, and lower neck region of the affected side may help considerably in most cases easing pain.

The exercises given in Chapters 17 and 18 (particularly exercises 10–14) together with those for postural correction and relaxation should be practised regularly. At first, there must be care in bending the head backwards, which, if it increases symptoms, should be omitted until the condition improves. Neck stress in bed must be avoided. Usually one pillow only is sufficient.

Similar conditions of spondylitis in the middle and lower-middle back may cause *intercostal neuritis,* with pains from the back following the line of the ribs to where they join the *sternum* (breast bone). As mentioned in Chapter 19, these pains may stimulate those of *angina pectoris,* in which case improvement under natural treatment may prove to be diagnostic, especially in the absence of other cardiac symptoms. The remedial exercises in Chapters 17 and 18 should be practised, in addition to exercises 1–5 and exercise 14.

In the lumbar region stiffness and pain may be called *lumbago* a term meaning only pain in that region of the back, whether affecting the soft tissues or joints or both.

The weight-bearing joints of the lower lumbar and pelvic (sacroiliac) joints need to be supported by correspondingly strong soft tissues, including muscles, ligaments and the intervertebral discs which cushion the spine and provide its flexibility. In too many cases modern civilised man's lack of regular exercise allows these important structures to weaken. Inevitably, sooner or later the heavier than usual weight has to be lifted or a jolt or a fall is suffered, which may cause strains and displacements of the lumbar or sacroiliac joints. In many other cases there may be no history of unusual or severe back strains or stresses. These may arise from chronic postural strains due to constant occupational stresses, or even to the use of slumpy chairs and saggy beds.

The so-called 'easy' chair may be far from easy in its effect on the spine and pelvis. All these joints may eventually develop varying degrees of spondylitis, and joint displacements will impose uneven pressures on the weakened discs which, by being distorted, may protrude to the point of pressing on the adjacent nerve roots (see Figures 8, 9 and 10), so as to cause the condition referred to as 'slipped disc'. More severe and incapacitating cases may result from the herniation of the disc with extrusion of the pulpy nucleus. The form of *neuritis* thus caused in the lower lumbar and sacral nerves is known as *sciatica* from its involvement with the *sciatic nerve,* which is the largest nerve in the body. Symptoms are similar to those of *brachial neuritis,* frequently with very severe pain.

Specialised manipulative techniques have long been omitted from the curriculums of the orthodox medical schools. In the distressing conditions described above, osteopathic or chiropractic techniques may be very helpful in correcting joint lesions and so relieving pressure on discs and nerve-roots. (See pp. 180-1 for how to contact qualified practitioner services.)

In acute low back and pelvic conditions, with or without sciatic symptoms, the treatment should be similar to that described for *brachial neuritis,* with fasting, balanced dietary and hot and cold fomentations which may considerably relieve pain. In severe cases the use of some form of pain-killer as a temporary measure may be inevitable, but complete suppression of pain may result in further damage if the limiting and guarding effect of pain, acting as nature's warning, is cancelled out with too powerful an analgesic. Also, it is generally true that the more effective a drug may be in suppressing pain, the more severe and dangerous are its side-effects.

Whenever possible, total bed-rest should be avoided – even relatively small movements help to avoid excessive weakening of muscles, etc. With any but the firmest of beds it will be helpful to insert a sheet of hardboard about 4 ft 6 in. (140 cm) long and slightly less than the width of the bed, between the mattress and the base of the bed.

As soon as possible exercises Nos. 1-7 (Chapter 17) and particularly Nos. 8 and 9 (Chapter 18), should be commenced, carefully at first and more vigorously as improvement is gained. It will be of lasting benefit to continue to perform this series of exercises as a regular habit; this will steadily improve the tensile strength and efficiency of the whole spinal musculature and so help to prevent recurrences. Thus, a few minutes daily will be well spent.

Concerning *traumatic arthritis* symptoms such as inflammation,

169

pain etc., may ease and disappear only to recur at some later date, when the old injury may prove to be susceptible to relatively moderate stresses and strains. However, long-term effects may be avoided if thorough treatment on nature-cure lines is carried out before a more chronic degenerative condition becomes established. This will apply even to athletes, whose fitness might be taken for granted, especially if there has been an accumulation of excess weight due to nutritional errors. Even in the later stages of such troubles the healing powers of repair compensation and adaptation may still perform 'slow miracles' if we cease to obstruct them and instead take action to assist the inborn 'healing effort of nature'. Osteopathy may be essential.

Another form of rheumatism, *gout,* is characterised by the depositing of uric acid and urates crystals in affected joints, often also with chalky deposits. Treatment should be commenced with the short fast, followed by strict adherence to the dietary as given in Chapter 14, Stage 1 and continuing with Stage 2 (Chapter 15.)

The dietary should be strictly vegetarian, with no meat, fish or poultry, as these foods in addition to other disadvantages, are sources of uric acid and other acidic toxins. Alcoholic drinks, especially the sweeter varieties, and all refined carbohydrate foods should be avoided.

Cold compresses should be applied to the affected joints at night, and hot and cold foot baths should be taken once daily. The bottom legs of the bed may be raised six or seven inches. Upward firm stroking of the leg muscles will help to decongest the feet and legs.

The Dangers of Smoking

The methods of self-treatment which have been described have dealt mainly with matters which are directly controllable by the sufferer. The further question arises as to how far and in which ways we are subject to adverse environmental factors. While some of these are at present beyond the control of the individual, there are others in which we do have a personal choice. One of these is the habit of smoking.

In 1954 the eminent doctors Sir Austin Bradford Hill and Professor Richard Doll published the findings of their researches which defined smoking as being the chief cause of cancer of the lung.

In a report (May 1969) to members of the British Safety Council, Dr Douglas Latto (Vice-Chairman of the Council) stated: 'There is no longer any room for doubt that smoking is the chief cause of cancer of the lung. In addition to lung cancer, cigarette smoking increases the chance of the following: cancer of the lip, larynx or oesophagus, bronchitis and emphysema, coronary thrombosis, cancer of the
170

bladder, peptic ulcer, gastric ulcer, duodenal ulcer.'

Smoking causes or worsens catarrhal conditions which in turn are closely associated with rheumatism and arthritis. The reports of Drs Hill and Doll have been confirmed by many leading health authorities. Following this, doctors have themselves given up smoking to a greater extent than have the general public, as a result of which while lung cancer has increased in the general public the disease amongst doctors has significantly decreased.

We are all familiar with the government warnings on cigarette packets but many still find it extremely hard to give up the habit.

What may help in this respect more than anything else is that with the adoption of the nature-cure way of life there will result a new quality of life, with a buoyancy of spirit, a lasting sense of well-being and a lessening of fears and frustrations and also in many cases with the ability to lead a fuller life, perhaps with new interests. All this will help to create an atmosphere in which the use of stimulants in an effort to create a temporary feeling of euphoria will no longer be needed. This may encourage and assist the victim's efforts to moderate or abandon these harmful habits which were associated with previous depression and nervous tension, so that he or she no longer needs cigarettes, 'pep' pills, or endless cups of tea and coffee to 'keep going'.

The dangers and disadvantages of drug treatment are very real – much greater than most people realise. The prevalence of iatrogenic disease is certainly much more serious than has so far been admitted. In these matters also the ultimate choice is with the individual.

The Hazards of Immunisation

Another hazardous practice is that of vaccination and inoculation for an increasing number of ailments. The validity of these artificial 'immunisations' (which, in fact, do not ensure immunity) has been questioned in Chapter 6. Perhaps the most valid criticism so far of these practices, was made in *The Hazards of Immunisation* by Sir Graham Wilson, who was formerly Director of the Public Health Laboratory Service, England and Wales. In addition to the many obvious cases of mortality and morbidity from these practices, Sir Graham Wilson states that there are also long-term hazards which are almost impossible to estimate fully or accurately.

Much more adverse evidence has been forthcoming since 1967, indicating the very real dangers, including brain damage, from whooping-cough vaccination.

Here, then, are further potentially dangerous and damaging environmental hazards with regard to which we may exercise a wide

171

measure of choice as to whether we submit ourselves and our children to these procedures.

Again, as in the case of rheumatoid arthritis, there are many instances of serious effects due to autoimmunity, in which the body attacks its own tissues. No valid explanation for these strange maladies has yet been advanced, but certainly it may well be one more example of the observation that nature, when attacked, 'always hits back'.

One thing of which we may be assured is that the fundamental natural methods herein described of treating our prevalent diseases are also the surest ways by which we may secure and maintain our natural resistance to disease and thus defend ourselves to some extent from many of the environmental hazards which at present are beyond our control. Meanwhile, we must encourage and help those environmental scientists whose task is to solve the many problems of pollution produced by the industrial civilisation in which we find ourselves.

Epilogue

In presenting the natural-therapy treatment for rheumatism and arthritis – the most widespread and prevalent group of diseases in modern industrial civilisation – I hope that readers will appreciate that similar methods are applicable to many other forms of illness. These methods are, in fact, the basis of the alternative school of medicine – nature's way to health – the need for which is now being realised as never before.

It must be accepted that health and disease are mutually exclusive. Thus, only by establishing the conditions for positive health will alternative medicine succeed as against the methods of symptom suppression which appear to be the main aim of orthodox medicine, motivated as it is by the high-pressure commercialism of the multinational drug houses. The fallacies of modern 'scientific medicine' have become apparent to a number of the most eminent doctors of the twentieth century. In 1935 Alexis Carrel (see p. 55) wrote:

We should ascertain whether natural resistance to infections could be conferred by definite conditions of life. Injections of specific vaccine or serum for each disease, repeated medical examinations of the whole population, construction of gigantic hospitals, are expensive and not very effective means of preventing diseases and of developing a nation's health. Good health should be natural. Such innate resistance gives the individual a strength, a boldness, which he does not possess when his survival depends on physicians.

Almost half a century later Professor Hywel Davies (University of Colorado Medical Centre), in his book *Modern Medicine - A Doctor's Dissent,* has written: 'There must be some risks involved in all treatment, but it is generally thought that in the practice of modern medicine the level of risk is acceptable in relation to the great benefits that follow. I do not find this to be so; in my view the risks to health are overall greater than is usually realised and the benefits are less. This applies specially to the use of drugs.'

Both of these authoritative writers have emphasised that health must be *natural* – it cannot be an artefact.

Dr Carrel wrote: 'Each individual has the power to modify his life to create around him an environment slightly different from that of the unthinking crowd.' He states further: 'This conception of natural health will meet with strong opposition because it disturbs our habits of thought.'

Furthermore, Dr Davies stated, 'Awareness of the potential for harm in the modern approach to drug therapy is by no means new: the pages of periodicals such as *Health for All** or *Nature's Way* have been replete with points of view reflecting this.' He added

The British National Health Service has been vaunted as the showpiece of Britain since its inception. Now almost bankrupt, ridden with dissatisfaction, strife and inefficiency – after 27 years there is nothing to suggest that the health of Britain has improved as a result of the advent of the NHS. The underlying fallacies are unexposed – namely that giant misconception that a rise in expenditure on 'Health' would lead to better health and a reduction therefore in the demand and cost; and perhaps the more basic misconception that the whole system contributes to health anyway.

The correctness of these statements is even more apparent in that for the year 1976 the cost of the NHS was more than £6,000 million.

What is more, there appears to be no evidence that private medicine is any more successful unless it manages to induce the patient to make necessary changes of habit and thus to play an active part in his own recovery; this is what naturopathy aims to do.

Dr Davies concluded: 'Changes in medicine there will be, and they will come in the main from public opinion.' A further criticism concerning modern scientific medicine's huge expenditure on research is the subject of a recent publication, *Paper Doctors,* by Vernon Coleman. Dr Coleman states: 'We have, over the last few years, spent hundreds of millions on searching for a cure for cancer. If we had spent that same amount of money on preventive medicine, designed to cut down the incidence of cancer, there is no doubt at all that a large number – probably half – of the people with cancer today would not have cancer.' Dr Coleman also quotes Macfarlane Burnet (Nobel prize winner, 1960) as stating: 'The contribution of laboratory science to medicine has virtually come to an end – almost none of modern basic research has any direct or indirect bearing on the prevention of disease or on the improvement of medical care' (*Genes, Dreams and Realities,* Medical and Technical Publishing Co., 1971).

A further consideration is that if the application of the measures of natural therapy becomes more widely practised there would be fewer cases referred to the surgeons for orthopaedic surgery, including the insertion of steel and plastic joints, all of which operations have their dangers and failures.

In the examples concerning the health and general freedom from disease among a number of isolated primitive peoples, including the Hunza (Chapter 9), the older members of the community, even the centenarians, were found to be healthy and fit, mentally active and in full possession of their faculties of sight, hearing, etc. We may expect that in our present civilisation the adoption of natural therapy, with the necessary changes in our faulty habits of life, would bring great benefits to individuals and to the community. Such benefits would include far fewer geriatric patients suffering from premature senility and merely existing in a state of 'medicated survival', thus helping to solve one of our major present-day problems.

* * *

Readers may find the following titles helpful and interesting.

Man, the Unknown by Alexis Carrel (Burnes & Oates, A. Clarke Books)

Nutrition and Health by Sir Robert McCarrison and H. M. Sinclair (Faber & Faber)

Relax Your Way to Health by Harold Cotton (Thorsons)

Need your Doctor be so Useless? by Andrew Malleson (George Allen & Unwin, 1973)

There's Gold in Them Thar Pills by Alan Klass (Penguin Special, 1975)

Modern Medicine - A Doctor's Dissent by Hywel Davies (Abelard, London)

Food for a Future by John Wynne-Tyson (Abacus Books, 1976)

An Outline of Naturopathic Psychotherapy by Milton Powell (British College of Naturopathy and Osteopathy, 6 Netherhall Gardens, London NW3 5RR)

Yoga and Health by Yesudian and Haich (Unwin Books, London)

* * *

Because of the importance of not submitting arthritic joints to undue strain, especially during the acute inflammatory stage, there are numerous aids of many types avilable. Even in the home, with simple matters such as turning taps, undoing the caps of tins and bottles, etc., the hands and wrists may suffer pain and/or damage. A list with illustrations and prices of such aids is available from the British Rheumatism and Arthritis Association, 6 Grosvenor Crescent, London SW1X 7ER (telephone 01-235 0902).

Also, a booklet entitled *Your Home and Your Rheumatism,* is published by The Arthritis and Rheumatism Council, 8-10 Charing Cross Road, London WC2 0HN. It gives some illustrations and an extensive list of aids, including simple garden tools, with names and addresses where each may be obtained.

* * *

In chapter 16 the desirability of obtaining organically grown produce is mentioned. Most health food stores do not stock fresh vegetables and fruit, but they may know if there is any farm or market garden in the vicinity from which such produce may be obtained.

Otherwise, information concerning such sources of supply may possibly be obtained from one or other of the following:

The Organic Food Finder and Directory (Rodale Press, Berkhamsted, Herts).

The OFS Directory of Growers and Producers, Organic Food Service, Ashe, Nr Brixham, Devon. This is free, so apply by letter enclosing postage for reply.

The Soil Association, Walnut Tree Manor, Haughley, Stowmarket, Suffolk.

Organic Farmers and Growers, Longridge, Greetings Road, Stowmarket, Suffolk.

The Henry Doubleday Research Association, Bocking, Braintree, Essex.

Those who have their own gardens, even the smallest earth patch, may grow some of their own fresh produce organically, using compost made from garden wastes, grass cuttings, and household wastes, etc., on the principle that what comes from the soil will go back to it. Straw, peat and plenty of seaweed may be used similarly. The physical work may be minimised (see reference below) – an important point with many rheumatics. Those who are not able to obtain seaweed may use a liquid seaweed, such as Maxicrop, or seaweed meal or granules.

Even on stone or concrete areas much may be grown in bottomless boxes made from old wood and filled with six inches or more of soil ('container gardening'). Even flat dwellers may grow some food for salads by means of the methods of sprouting seeds. A folder giving a list of many suitable seeds, complete with recipes, is published by Thomson and Morgan Seedsmen, London Road, Ipswich IP2 0BA. Most health food stores, stock a variety of seeds, including beans, for sprouting.

Further recommended reading:

The No-work Gardening Book, by Ruth Stout and Richard Clemence (White Lion Publishers, London)

Seaweed in Agriculture and Horticulture by W. A. Stephenson (EP Publishing, East Ardley, Wakefield, Yorks.)

*   *   *

Concerning the need for aids as noted on p. 175 it may be asked why such aids may be necessary if natural treatment is effective. The answer is that in the severe, acute condition there is need for care in not overstraining the severely affected joints. In point of fact, the orthodox treatment with drugs which suppress pain and inflammation tends to obscure nature's warning and in this way possibly inducing the sufferer to submit the affected joints to undesirable stress at a stage when the usual signs of weakness and pain would ensure more rational care.

This was exemplified on the introduction of steroid treatments, when under the influence of the drugs the sufferer was temporarily able to perform hitherto impossible exertions which would normally be inhibited by the natural effect of pain.

176

Further examples have been provided by athletes who may have severely strained a knee or other joint and who have received pain-killing injections enabling them at once to carry on with their exertions against all the dictates of nature; this may result in irreparable damage to the affected joints.

Therefore, certain mechanical aids which minimise stress on acutely affected joints may be of great temporary assistance. With the help of natural therapy, however, the needs for such aids may soon be reduced. This prospect will encourage sufferers to persist with the measures of self-help herein described, and by means of these procedures restore the heritage of health and remove the real causes of disease, thus promoting healing and repair of affected tissues and also benefiting the whole human organism.

The statement that 'only nature heals' is as true nowadays as it was in the days of Hippocrates. Thus, nature cure may be regarded as a practical exercise in human ecology – the study of man's relationship to his whole environment, both internal and external.

Perhaps the most convincing support for the above statements may be seen in the condition in which the National Health Service finds itself. This was well expressed in *The Radio Times,* which announcing a 1977 programme in the series *Horizon* entitled 'The Trouble with Medicine', stated:

Each year medicine gets more expensive – last year the NHS cost us over £6,000 million. Yet more money does not seem to bring better health. Today a middle-aged man has little greater expectancy of life than his great-great grandfather 100 years ago. Medicine has failed to conquer diseases like cancer and heart disease which continue to increase.

This statement may well be extended to include rheumatism and arthritis. *The Radio Times* continued: . . . 'if the health problems of today are to be overcome the role of medicine will have to be redefined.'

In writing this book I have sought to provide some necessary guidance, based on personal experience, for those seeking to find and follow the direct path to better health.

It would be incorrect to refer to the system of treatment herein described as 'fringe medicine'. A more appropriate term in the circumstances of today could be 'alternative medicine'. It is, however, based on fundamental principles, both in theory and practice, which are the ultimate determinants of health.

Summary of Treatment Programme

The following summary is intended to provide a readily accessible programme of treatment which may be referred to from day to day by those carrying out the recommended course of self-treatment.

It cannot be stressed too strongly, however, that a clear understanding of the aims and objectives of the various treatment measures is absolutely essential if they are to be applied effectively. Therefore, the reader is urged to review frequently the relevant sections of this book, especially those indicated by the page references shown against each item listed in the summary.

Prior to commencing the course, the reader should familiarise himself or herself with the following techniques and remedial measures so that they can be readily co-ordinated into the daily timetable as economically as possible.

1 Relaxing Muscle Tension

Test for tension pp. 123–5
Relaxation technique pp. 126–7, 134

2 Remedial Exercises

Deep-breathing exercises Nos 1–5 pp. 127–33
Spinal exercises Nos 6–14 pp. 140–9
Postural correction exercise No. 15 pp. 149–52
Active outdoor exercise p. 153
Each exercise should be repeated from five to ten times but care should be taken to avoid undue fatigue or strain.

3 Relieving Pain and Reducing Swelling

Compresses and baths pp. 163–5

Dietetic Treatment Programme

Stage 1

(a) Days 1–2 (p. 95)

From four to five ounces of fresh ripe grapes at usual mealtimes – no drinks or other foods.

(b) Days 3–9 (pp. 95–6)
    On rising   Small tumbler of carrot and fruit juice
    Breakfast   Any two kinds of ripe raw fruit
    Mid-morning   Hot yeast drink
    Mid-day   Raw salad with oil and lemon dressing etc., and cheese followed by raw fruit.
    Evening   Raw fruit and yogurt
    Drink   Carrot and fruit juice or yeast drink, medium tumbler.

Stage 2

Days 1–14 (pp. 105–7)
    On rising   Tumbler of fruit and vegetable juices
    Breakfast   Three tablespoons muesli with one tablespoon bran, moistened with milk
    or any two kinds of ripe raw fruit
    or dried fruit with one tablespoon wheat-germ
    Mid-morning   Hot yeast drink
    First main meal   Raw salad with 2oz cheese or a hard-boiled egg, dressed with yogurt or oil and lemon dressing. Two slices of crispbread or wholemeal bread with butter or margarine. Ripe raw fruit, or fresh fruit salad, or up to half pint yogurt.
    Mid-afternoon   Small tumbler unsweetened fruit juice, or cup of unsweetened weak tea.
    Second main meal   Cooked vegetables with poached egg or up to 2 oz grated cheese, or up to 8 walnuts, or vegetable protein.
Baked apple with raisins, or as first main meal (but do not repeat any one dish on same day).
    Late evening   Small tumbler unsweetened fruit or vegetable juice
    Note: The first and second main meals may be interchanged.

Stage 3

Days 1–23 + (p. 108)
    Repeat complete programme, Stages 1 and 2, days 1–23+.

Stage 4

Days 1–2 or 3 (p. 109)

No food of any kind. Small tumbler vegetable and fruit juices every two or three hours throughout day.

Day 3 or 4 (pp. 95–6)
Fresh raw fruit only (any two kinds) at usual mealtimes, with juices or yeast drink as desired.

Days 4 or 5–7 (pp. 95–6)
Dietary regime as for days 3–9 stage 1.

Stage 5 (pp. 109–10)

Continue as stage 2, interspersed with stage 4 (days 1–7) at intervals of from 4 to 6 weeks.

It will be noted that stages 1–4 cover a period of some 52 days, after which stage 5 constitutes a continuing health-building regime interspersed with 'booster' repetitions of stage 4.

The latter should also be implemented should a 'healing crisis' occur (see pp. 118–20).

Patience and perseverance must be exercised in attempting to eradicate chronic and deep-seated conditions such as arthritis and other rheumatic disorders, and it should be remembered that the rate and degree of recovery will usually be related to such factors as the patient's age and general health, the severity and duration of the symptoms, and the nature of any previous medical treatment.

For guidance in planning subsequent dietary see *Every Woman's Wholefood Cook Book* by Vivien and Clifford Quick (Thorsons Publishers Ltd).

For those who wish to seek a qualified practitioner for further advice and/or treatment, graduates of the following schools must have completed a four-year full-time course and qualified by examination:

The British College of Naturopathy and Osteopathy, Frazer House, 6 Netherhall Gardens, London NW3 5RR Tel: 01 435 7830
Diplomas in Naturopathy and Osteopathy

The British School of Osteopathy, 16 Buckingham Gate, London SW1 Tel: 01 828 9479
Diplomas in Osteopathy

The Anglo-European College of Chiropractic,
1 Cavendish Road, Bournemouth BH1 1RA
Tel: Bournemouth 24777
Diplomas in Chiropractic

Bibliography

Diabetes, Coronary Thrombosis, and the Saccharine Disease, Cleave, Campbell and Painter (John Wright & Sons, Bristol, 1969)

Every Woman's Wholefood Cook Book, Vivien and Clifford Quick (Thorsons Publishers Ltd, 1974)

Food for a Future, Jon Wynne-Tyson (Abacus Books, 1976)

Genes, Dreams and Realities, Macfarlane Burnet (Medical & Technical Publishing Co., 1971)

The Hazards of Immunization, Sir Graham Wilson (Athlone Press, 1967)

Health and the Environment, John Lenihan and William Fletcher (eds) (Blackie, 1976).

Man Adapting, René Dubos (Yale University Press, 1965).

Man, Medicine and Environment, René Dubos (Encylopaedia Britannica, Inc., 1968; Pelican Books, 1970)

Man the Unknown, Alexis Carrel (first published 1935; Pelican Books, 1948).

Medical Nemesis, Ivan Illich (Calder & Boyars, 1975).

Modern Medicine – A Doctor's Dissent, Hywel Davies (Abelard-Schuman, London 1977).

My Water Cure, Sebastian Kneipp (first published 1893; Thorsons Publishers Ltd, 1979).

Need Your Doctor Be So Useless, Andrew Malleson (George Allen & Unwin, 1973).

The No-work Garden Book, Ruth Stout and Richard Clemence (White Lion Publishers, London, 1976).

Nutrition and Health, R. McCarrison and H. M. Sinclair (Faber & Faber, 3rd edn 1961).

Nutrition and Physical Degeneration, Weston A. Price (American Academy of Applied Nutrition, 5th impression 1950).

Our Polluted Food, Jack Lucas (Charles Knight, 1975).

An Outline of Naturopathic Psychotherapy, Milton Powell (The British College of Naturopathy and Osteopathy, 6 Netherhall Gardens, London NW3 5RR, by post £1.20).

Paper Doctors, Vernon Coleman (Temple Smith, 1977).

Relax Your Way to Health, Harold Cotton (Thorsons Publishers Ltd).

Rheumatism and Arthritis in Britain, (Office of Health Economics, London, 1973).

The Saccharine Disease, T. L. Cleave (John Wright & Sons, Bristol, 1974).

Seaweed in Agriculture and Horticulture, W. A. Stephenson (EP Publishing, East Ardley, Wakefield, Yorks., 2nd edition 1973).

The Side Effects of Drugs: a Survey of Unwanted Effects of Drugs 1972–5, (excerpts) (Medica Publishing Co., 1976).

The Stress of Life, Hans Selye (Longman, 1957).

There's Gold in Them Thar Pills, Arnold Klass (Penguin Special, 1975).

182

The Wisdom of the Body, Walter Cannon (W. W. Norton, 1932; Kegan Paul, Trench, Trubner, 1934).

Yoga and Health, Yesudian and Haich (George Allen & Unwin, 1953; Unwin Paperbacks, 1976).

Index

186

187